Paul Turner

WHEN OTHER CHRISTIANS BECOME CATHOLIC

A PUEBLO BOOK

Liturgical Press   Collegeville, Minnesota

www.litpress.org

A Pueblo Book published by Liturgical Press

Cover design by David Manahan, o.s.b. Illustration by Frank Kacmarcik, Obl.S.B., "The holy city, the new Jerusalem" in Revelation.

Library of Congress Cataloging-in-Publication Data

Turner, Paul, 1953–
    When other Christians become Catholic / Paul Turner.
       p. cm.
    "A Pueblo book."
    Includes bibliographical references and index.
    ISBN-13: 978-0-8146-6216-8
    ISBN-10: 0-8146-6216-1
       1. Catholic converts.   2. Conversion—Catholic Church.   3. Catholic Church—Membership.   I. Title.
    BX4668.15
    248.2'42—dc22
                                                                    2006025970

"No one working in any facet of the Rites of Christian Initiation of Adults in today's churches can afford to miss this book! Clearly and succinctly written, Paul Turner underscores that the RCIA is not about making 'converts' out of baptized Christians from other traditions but was intended to be and should be still about the way in which unbaptized people are fully initiated into Christ and the Church. Hence, this study explores in an ecumenically sensitive way what our common baptism means with regard to rites of reception into full communion."

— Maxwell Johnson
University of Notre Dame

"Baptism makes it different! Beware when you read this book! It will change how you implement the Initiation process in your parish. Paul Turner has once again given the Church a masterful book to help all of us understand Baptism and in particular how we are to walk with those who approach the Catholic Church for 'union and communion.' Besides a comprehensive historical grasp of the development of the Rite of Reception into the Catholic Faith, he also provides practical insights and direction for those involved in today's initiation ministry with candidates for reception into full communion of the Catholic Church."

— Sr. Gael Gensler, o.s.f.
St. Julie Billiart Parish
Tinley Park, Illinois

"Tradition is not the past but the Church's present understanding of the dynamic treasure its past has transmitted. Authored by one who is both scholar and pastor, this book on a hitherto neglected area of pastoral liturgy opens up for the reader the riches of that tradition in a way that makes them relevant for today. Paul Turner's illuminating analysis of the multiple problems implicit in the formation of liturgical rites, past and present, demonstrates that change has always been the law of Catholic liturgy, and that Catholic rites modified in the aftermath of Vatican II were themselves also the product of growth and change to express new understandings and meet new needs. The new rites for receiving baptized Christians into full communion with the Catholic Church are delineated clearly and critically, with special emphasis on problems peculiar to their American adaptation and use. Read this book and you'll wish Paul Turner were your pastor."

— Robert F. Taft, s.j.
Pontifical Oriental Institute, Rome

Contents

IN MEMORIAM

IACOBI DVNNING

DE CATECVMENATV FORI AMERICANI
SEPTENTRIONALIS CONDITORIS

QVI AB INITIIS

AVCTORI COMPREHENSIS HOC IN
VOLVMEN DE PROPOSITIS RESTITIT

ET VLTERIVS

PASSIONEM EIVS BAPTISMI PRO
SACRAMENTO INFLAMMAVIT

GRATA ECCLESIA

I wish to thank

Dale Sieverding, who researched

The Centro Pro Unione, which hopes

Sant' Anselmo, which stored

The Casa Santa Maria, which hosted

Maxwell Johnson and Gael Gensler, who read

John Huels, who clarified

The North American Academy of Liturgy, which affirmed

Thomas Sullivan and Jerome Werth, who assisted

St. Munchin and St. Aloysius, who interceded

And God, who brings us to birth

P.T.

Acknowledgments

Excerpts from the English translation of *Rite of Christian Initiation of Adults* © 1985, International Committee on English in the Liturgy, Inc. (ICEL). All rights reserved.

Excerpt from *Journey to the Fullness of Life* © 2000, (USCCB). Excerpt from "The Reception of Baptized Christians and the Rite of Baptism During the Easter Vigil" © 1977, (USCCB). Excerpt from *Catechism of the Catholic Church* © 1994, (USCCB).

Excerpts from the *Code of Canon Law* are reprinted with the permission of the Canon Law Society of America, Washington, DC.

Excerpts from several Vatican documents and from *Dominus Iesus* are reprinted with permission from Libreria Editrice Vaticana.

Excerpts from *One at the Table: The Reception of Baptized Christians*, ed. Ronald A. Oakham (Chicago: Liturgy Training Publications, 1995). Reprinted with permission.

Excerpts from James Dunning's "What Is a Catechized Adult?" are from *Forum Newsletter* 9, no. 3 (Summer, 1992) 1, 4, 6. Published by North American Forum on the Catechumenate (www.naforum.org). Used with permission.

Excerpts from John Huels' *Liturgy and Law* are used with permission.

Part I

Not the Beginning

Chapter 1

Baptized Christians

THE NEED

A baptized Christian who becomes a Catholic makes a personal decision with far-reaching implications. The motivation for changing from one Christian family to another may be as practical as fusing one household's diverse worship habits, or as spiritual as deepening one's experience of God. The result is one small step in the global dance of Christian unity. The decision may exact an emotional cost on family and friends in the previous church of baptism. Yet it brings peace of heart to the individual, the family, and friends in the subsequent church of destination.

Many people choose a religion different from the one they first knew. Some change several times. In parts of the world where the splinters of Christianity are manifest, the baptized who seek to become Catholic may outnumber the unbaptized who desire initiation.

Global records are not available. The Vatican publishes the number of baptisms in each diocese worldwide, but it does not distinguish adult from infant baptisms, nor does it publish the worldwide number of receptions of those already baptized.[1]

However, such statistics are available in the United States, where 52 percent of those becoming Catholic are previously baptized adults (see Table on page 4).[2]

---

[1] *Annuarium Statisticum Ecclesiae and Annuario Pontificio* (Vatican City: Libreria Editrice Vaticana).

[2] Chart compiled by author with statistics taken from *The Official Catholic Directory* (New York: PJ Kenedy) 1995–2005. The same reports show over a million infant baptisms in the Catholic Church each year.

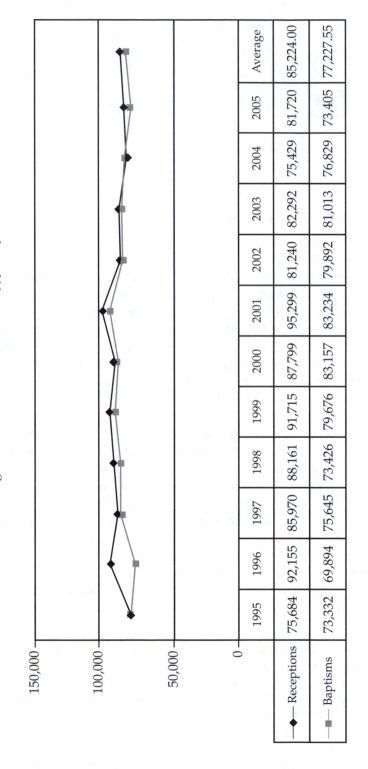

Totals of Previously Baptized Adults (Receptions) and Unbaptized Adults (Baptisms) Becoming Catholic in the United States 1995–2005

	1995	1996	1997	1998	1999	2000	2001	2002	2003	2004	2005	Average
Receptions	75,684	92,155	85,970	88,161	91,715	87,799	95,299	81,240	82,292	75,429	81,720	85,224.00
Baptisms	73,332	69,894	75,645	73,426	79,676	83,157	83,234	79,892	81,013	76,829	73,405	77,227.55

On average, over 77,000 adults are baptized each year in the Catholic Church: and over 85,000 baptized in other Christians churches become Catholic. The preparation of all these candidates falls to Catholic parishes, where ministers rely on the Rite of Christian Initiation of Adults (RCIA)—a work that gives far more attention to the unbaptized than it does to the baptized—for direction.

The RCIA also addresses the needs of Catholics who were baptized in infancy but never received adequate catechesis, confirmation, and/or first communion. This book, however, is primarily about those baptized in other Christian churches who later become Catholic.

There are many reasons why people decide to become Catholic. In the United States, a pre-millennial survey of catechumens and baptized candidates summarized the motives this way:

> Responses indicate that the individuals' main motivation for participating in the RCIA is to unify an ecumenical or interchurch marriage. Of married participants, 83 percent have Catholic spouses. Participants' second strongest motivation reportedly is a spiritual need and hunger, most often related to family life, health (of oneself or a loved one), a death of a loved one, a feeling of emptiness, or an inspiring experience. The third strongest motivation cited is a feeling of loneliness or a need for an authentic community. These motivations are often combined, and many persons mention more than one.[3]

In many Catholic parishes, the primary reason people become interested in joining the church is their marriage and family life. The number of Catholics who marry someone of another faith has grown; marriage has become a tool for evangelization. Even if someone becomes interested in the church primarily because of a Catholic spouse, other motives usually ripen. It is not uncommon to hear a candidate for reception say something like this: "I started this for my spouse, but I'm sticking with it for me."

Parish ministers discover that the religious experience of previously baptized candidates is not uniform. Some have virtually no religious upbringing. Others have been active in the church of their baptism for years. Some have never read from the Bible; others know it well. Still

---

[3] *Journey to the Fullness of Life* (Washington DC: United States Conference of Catholic Bishops, 2000) 7.

others have been faithfully attending Sunday Mass with a Catholic spouse and participating in parish apostolates for decades. Occasionally, churchgoers are surprised to learn that someone with whom they worship every week is not a Catholic.

Parish ministers sort through the motives, offer catechetical formation, discern the readiness of those who express a desire for membership, and celebrate with them the rite of reception. In doing so, parish ministers are, at a local level, fulfilling a great need of the universal church.

THE RITUAL TEXT

The title of the appropriate rite is the Reception of Baptized Christians into the Full Communion of the Catholic Church. A fruit of the Second Vatican Council, it has no precise predecessor. Previously, baptized Christians were received into the Catholic Church by professing faith in the church, renouncing heresy, and undergoing a conditional baptism, while the priest supplied the rites omitted from their original baptism.

Introduction

The introduction to the rite of reception explains its purpose:

> This is the liturgical rite by which a person born and baptized in a separated ecclesial Community is received, according to the Latin rite, into the full communion of the Catholic Church. The rite is so arranged that no greater burden than necessary (see Acts 15:28) is required for the establishment of communion and unity.[4]

This introduction says the rite pertains to those "born and baptized" in an ecclesial community separated from the Catholic Church. This presumes the candidate was baptized as an infant. But the rite applies to one who was baptized later in life as well. The circumstances of one's birth do not matter as much as the church of one's baptism.

The rite uses the phrase "a separated ecclesial Community" to designate one with a valid baptism but not sharing the full communion of the Catholic Church. The Catholic Church recognizes the baptisms

---

[4] *Rite of Christian Initiation of Adults*, Study Edition, Prepared by International Committee on English in the Liturgy (Collegeville, MN: Liturgical Press, 1988) 473.

of mainline Christian bodies, but it does not share communion with them. Ministers in many Christian churches offer communion to visiting Catholics, but the Catholic Church does not return such an invitation to visiting Christians. Nor does the Catholic Church permit its members to receive communion when they attend services at another Christian church.[5]

The rite is about being "received"—not forgiven or reconciled. The reception admits the person into "the full communion" of the Catholic Church, with the privilege of sharing the Eucharist.

Due to the influence of the ecumenical movement, the rite was simplified so that "communion and unity"—the goals of the rite—could be accomplished with "no greater burden than necessary." This paragraph cites several documents of the Second Vatican Council[6] and a passage from Acts of the Apostles.[7] The allusion to Acts is from the so-called Council of Jerusalem, where the apostles debated the requirements for Gentiles to become Christian. Those who thought Gentiles should first become Jews lost under the rubric that the Gentiles should be baptized with no greater burden than necessary.[8]

That was the spirit behind the creation of the rite of reception. It was intended to downplay the ceremony in order to affirm the baptism already received. "Any appearance of triumphalism should be carefully avoided."[9] And, "Anything that would equate candidates for reception with those who are catechumens is to be absolutely avoided."[10]

The rite envisions that the candidate has already been appropriately prepared in mind and heart. "The baptized Christian is to receive both doctrinal and spiritual preparation, adapted to individual pastoral

---

[5] Pontifical Council for Promoting Christian Unity, *Directory for the Application of Principles and Norms on Ecumenism* (Vatican City, 1993) 130–132.

[6] Constitution on the Liturgy, *Sacrosanctum concilium*, art. 69b; Decree on Ecumenism *Unitatis redintegratio*, nos. 3 and 18. It also cites the postconciliar text from the Secretariat for Christian Unity, *Ecumenical Directory I*, no. 19: *Acta Apostolicæ Sedæ* 59 (1967) 581.

[7] Acts 15:28.

[8] Otherwise, Gentiles would have to have been circumcised before becoming Christian. A matter of more concern for Gentile men, the argument was lost amid Christianity's newfound freedom from the old law.

[9] RCIA 475.

[10] RCIA 477.

requirements."[11] These "individual pastoral requirements" suggest that the framers of the rite did not envision a circumstance when several or very many candidates would be prepared together. The rite itself is composed with the intention of receiving one single candidate.[12]

Thus the introduction to the rite envisions a simple ceremony with a profound meaning: A previously baptized person, having prepared for this day in mind and heart, is received into the Catholic Church at a celebration with a local Catholic community.

Sponsors

To assist with the preparation, the candidate receives a sponsor. The sponsor also plays a role in the rite:

> At the reception, the candidate should be accompanied by a sponsor and may even have two sponsors. If someone has had the principal part in guiding or preparing the candidate, he or she should be the sponsor.[13]

The Catholic Church acknowledges three different occasions for sponsors: the catechumenate, deferred confirmation, and the rite of reception.

- When a catechumen begins formation, a sponsor assists. This sponsor may serve as the godparent for baptism and confirmation, but need not; someone else may fill that role.[14]

- When a child is baptized, he or she receives one or two godparents, and when the child is later confirmed, someone serves as the sponsor. Ideally, a baptismal godparent serves again as the confirmation sponsor,[15] though this is rarely observed.

---

[11] Ibid.

[12] The English translation is not consistent on this point. See, for example, the description of the homily, in which "the celebrant should express gratitude to God for those being received and allude to their own baptism as the basis for their reception . . . and to the eucharist, which for the first time they will celebrate with the Catholic community" (RCIA 489). All those plurals are in the singular in the *editio typica*.

[13] RCIA 483.

[14] RCIA 10.

[15] Code of Canon Law, hereafter CCL (Washington DC: Canon Law Society of America, 1983) 893/2.

- When a baptized Christian is received into the Catholic Church, a sponsor assists. If confirmation is administered, the same person logically becomes the confirmation sponsor.

The Code of Canon Law, however, gives no information about a sponsor for reception. The canonical requirements for confirmation sponsors are the same as those for godparents at baptism.[16] The same requirements would likely apply for the sponsor for reception. In the relevant text, the code uses the English word "sponsor" for the baptismal godparent, which is confusing. But the requirements for godparents and sponsors are the same:

> To be permitted to take on the function of sponsor a person must . . . have completed the sixteenth year of age, unless the diocesan bishop has established another age, or the pastor or minister has granted an exception for a just cause; be a Catholic who has been confirmed and has already received the most holy sacrament of the Eucharist and who leads a life of faith in keeping with the function to be taken on; [and] not be bound by any canonical penalty legitimately imposed or declared.[17]

Presumably, at the time of baptism, the individual received one or two godparents from his or her own local church community. Those godparent relationships remain intact. Thus the baptized Christian who becomes Catholic receives a sponsor—and not a godparent—from the Catholic community.

The specific duties of a sponsor for reception are nowhere explained. In practice, a sponsor is often a person who represents the local community, who has made an impression on the candidate, who sets an example of Catholic life, who will assist in the rite of reception, and who will help integrate the newly received Catholic into the community.

It often seems that the logical person is the Catholic spouse. After all, many Christians become Catholic because of the spouse's inspiration. The law does not forbid the Catholic spouse from being the sponsor, but many parishes discourage it. The spouse already has a role. The

---

[16] "To perform the function of [confirmation] sponsor, a person must fulfill the conditions mentioned in can. 874." CCL 893/1.

[17] CCL 874/1.

sponsor represents the care of the broader faith community beyond the family.

Structure

The rite of reception unfolds simply, ideally during a Mass at any time of year. If the reception takes place apart from a solemnity (for example a holy day of obligation) or a Sunday, the readings and prayers may be taken from the Mass "For the Unity of Christians" from the Masses for Various Needs and Occasions.[18] After the homily, the celebrant invites the candidate to come forward with his or her sponsor. All the faithful, together with the candidate and sponsor, recite the Nicene Creed. This shows the unity of baptismal faith already shared between the candidate and the Catholic community.

The one being received adds this profession of faith: "I believe and profess all that the holy Catholic Church believes, teaches, and proclaims to be revealed by God."[19] The statement is simple and direct.

The celebrant calls the candidate by name and makes the statement known as the Act of Reception:

> N., the Lord receives you into the Catholic Church. His loving kindness has led you here, so that in the unity of the Holy Spirit you may have full communion with us in the faith that you have professed in the presence of his family.[20]

The celebrant administers the sacrament of confirmation, unless the person is coming from a church with a confirmation recognized by the Catholic Church.[21] Then the celebrant "takes the hands of the newly received person into his own as a sign of friendship and acceptance."[22] The local bishop may permit the substitution of another gesture. The meaning of the gesture appears right in the rubrics—*signum amicalis*

---

[18] RCIA 487.

[19] RCIA 491.

[20] RCIA 492.

[21] For example, the Catholic Church recognizes the confirmations of the Orthodox Church, the Old Catholic Church, and the Society of St. Pius X. It does not recognize the confirmations of the Protestant-Anglican traditions because the Catholic Church believes they do not have valid ordinations, which are required for the valid administration of this sacrament.

[22] RCIA 495.

receptionis—a sign of a friendly welcome. The rubrics rarely explain the meaning of the rites, but this gesture is new and unique.

The general intercessions follow, and then the entire assembly may be invited to "greet the newly received person in a friendly manner."[23] This may replace the sign of peace during the communion rite of the Mass, but its function is slightly different. This is meant to be a friendly greeting—*omnes amicaliter salutant*—not precisely the exchange of peace and unity that leads to the sacramental communion of the faithful.

The Mass continues, and the newly received person shares in communion for the first time, preferably under both kinds.[24]

That is how the rite progresses, but it is rarely celebrated that way in the United States, where it is more common to see this liturgy folded into the Easter Vigil. In that setting it takes on a grander dimension, as a group of baptized candidates joins the group of the unbaptized in an expansive celebration. The preparation for the rite of reception has also become more complex. Due to large numbers, candidates in many parishes are often prepared together with those who are unbaptized, with the assumption that everyone needs the same catechesis. The pastoral practice has drifted, then, from the council's original intent.

THE ECCLESIAL CONTEXT

The ritual text has an ecclesial context. In preparing candidates for reception, parishes involve them in a multilayered formation including catechesis, service, community life, preliminary rites, and spiritual guidance. The spiritual formation of candidates is paced by rituals preceding their reception.

Rites Preceding Reception

In the United States baptized candidates are invited to participate in a number of rituals that precede their reception. The American edition of the rite of reception (Part II, section 5 of the Rite of Christian Initiation of Adults) explains:

> During the period of their doctrinal and spiritual preparation individual candidates for reception into the full communion of the

[23] RCIA 497.
[24] RCIA 498.

Catholic Church may benefit from the celebration of liturgical rites marking their progress in formation. Thus, for pastoral reasons and in light of the catechesis in the faith which these baptized Christians have received previously, one or several of the rites included in Part II, 4—"Preparation of Uncatechized Adults for Confirmation and Eucharist"—may be celebrated as they are presented or in similar words. In all cases, however, discernment should be made regarding the length of catechetical formation required for each individual candidate for reception into the full communion of the Catholic Church.[25]

Part II, section 4 includes a series of rites created in the United States, patterned on the rites preparatory for adult baptism but adapted for those who are already baptized. The forgoing paragraph appears in the American edition of section 5, the introduction to the rite of reception, and it permits the celebration of the section 4 rites "for pastoral reasons and in light of the catechesis" the candidates have already received. But section 4 pertains to the preparation of *uncatechized* adults.

Still, section 5 says, "the length of catechetical formation required for each individual candidate for reception" needs to be determined. This allows parishes to judge whether or not to use these adapted rites for candidates case by case. This was important to state because the original universal text for the rite of reception merely says in its introduction, "During the period of preparation the candidate may share in worship in conformity with the provisions of the *Ecumenical Directory*."[26] At its simplest, this meant that candidates could attend Sunday Mass but not receive communion; the directory also permits other forms of common Christian worship.[27]

Prior to the rite of reception, then, the universal text envisions that the candidate will participate in Catholic worship—except for receiving communion. But the American edition introduced a series of rites to mark previously undefined stages along the way to one's reception. These stages were conceived for those who were uncatechized, but they have been widely used for any baptized candidate.

[25] RCIA 478.

[26] RCIA 477.

[27] *Directorium ad ea quae a Concilio Vaticano Secundo de re oecumenica promulgata sunt exsequenda: Ad totam ecclesiam*, Acta Apostolicae Sedis [AAS] 59 (1967) 583–592.

In 1986 the National Conference of Catholic Bishops distinguished between those baptized persons who "have received relatively little Christian upbringing" and those "who have lived as Christians." It was envisioned that the program of catechetical formation—both doctrinal and spiritual—would be different for each group.[28] In practice, though, many Catholic parishes assume that baptized candidates in formation for reception are thereby uncatechized, so they celebrate with them the adapted rites.

Spiritual Formation as Conversion

The rite does not place greater importance on either doctrinal or spiritual formation. But some theologians have offered reflections on this point. Rita Ferrone, for example, indicates that doctrinal apprehension and spiritual growth are just two of three movements happening to those joining Catholicism from another ecclesial community. She adds to them the gifts the candidate brings to the Catholic Church. Of these three, she states that spiritual growth holds priority:

> The call to holiness, to conversion, must be considered the first priority of all the activity surrounding reception. It reigns over and, if necessary, supersedes the other two movements we have just considered, because a just appreciation of the gifts of Catholicism and a true willingness to share from the storehouse of one's spiritual history demand a chastened self-awareness, humility, patience and all the spiritual gifts that come from God.[29]

Going a step further, Ron Oakham argues that the candidate is undergoing a conversion, and hence the experience is paschal. He cites the introduction to the Rite of Christian Initiation of Adults, which states, "The whole initiation must bear a markedly paschal character."[30]

> This "paschal character" is most often spoken of throughout the ritual text with the term *conversion*. . . . [T]he initiation process must first and foremost seek to foster the conversion going on

[28] National Statutes for the Catechumenate 31 (see Appendix III of RCIA).

[29] Rita Ferrone, "Reception in Context: Historical, Theological and Pastoral Reflections," in *One at the Table: The Reception of Baptized Christians*, ed. Ronald A. Oakham (Chicago: Liturgy Training Publications, 1995) 38.

[30] RCIA 8.

within the person's life. . . . The task of the initiation minister is not just to educate the candidate about Catholicism but to discern, along with the candidate, what it is that God is prompting in his or her life.[31]

Oakham believes this same sense of conversion guides the spiritual formation of candidates for reception, even though they are already baptized.

This view fits with the second presentation of the rite of reception in the American edition of the Rite of Christian Initiation of Adults.[32] There, the rite appears not on its own but combined with adult baptism at the Easter Vigil. This form has become so common in Catholic parishes that many Catholics who prepare adults for membership are unaware that baptized candidates may be received another way. The combined rite at the Easter Vigil has fostered the common preparation of baptized candidates and unbaptized catechumens, subsumed into the same doctrinal and spiritual formation. By adopting Easter as the paradigmatic occasion for celebrating the rite of reception, the Catholic Church in the United States has reframed the meaning of the rite and its attendant preparation into something more resembling a conversion, a dying and a rising—rather than an evolution, a coming to full communion. Everyone has multiple experiences in life that convert them from one way of thinking to another, but foundational in the context of initiation is the conversion to Christ represented by baptism. All other conversions are secondary by comparison.

Contextualization in the Easter Vigil has caused the simple rite of reception envisioned by the council to morph into a grand celebration on the most important night of the liturgical calendar. This happened as part of an enthusiastic response to the restored catechumenate in a nation where baptized candidates for reception outnumbered catechumens. However, the decision was costly in terms of understanding the distinct meaning of these rites.

Oakham recounts a conversation that has been replayed with different characters in many other parishes. He had adapted the

[31] Ron Oakham, "Normative Dimensions of Initiation," in *One at the Table*, 72–73.

[32] Celebration at the Easter Vigil of the Sacraments of Initiation and of the Rite of Reception into the Full Communion of the Catholic Church, RCIA 562–94.

prebaptismal scrutinies to include baptized candidates for reception. A candidate named Mark reflected on the rituals of initiation. Oakham writes,

> He concluded his comments with what I found to be an unnerving statement: "It all leaves me wishing I hadn't already been baptized; then I could be baptized at the Easter Vigil."
> Like neon blazing in the night, our failure flashed before me. In working to help Mark develop his faith life as a Catholic Christian, we unconsciously had diminished his respect for his baptism.[33]

Such a conversation is a symptom that something has gone wrong with the rite of reception. The council envisioned an ecumenically sensitive rite that would promote the concept of one baptism among Christians. But the rite of reception is being celebrated as a near equivalent with the initiation of the unbaptized.

Joseph A. Favazza thinks of candidates for reception as "embodied seasons of Advent." He explains:

> Something wonderful has already happened, yet we await it afresh. They are the "already but not yet," incarnated reminders of a world full of grace and yearning for fulfillment.[34]

If baptism is a beginning, the rite of reception is not. It meets people midstream in the Christian crossing. Celebrating the rite of reception with integrity requires a unique spiritual formation distinct from the prebaptismal catechumenate. Preparation for it begins in the middle of life in Christ, not at the beginning. A deeper understanding of the rite of reception will lead to a more meaningful preparation and a more expressive celebration. This rite grasps each candidate by the hand, wherever he or she is in the stream of Christianity, and brings them safely ashore.

The next part of this book will summarize the liturgical, theological, and ecumenical climate that led to the creation of the rite of reception. The final part will investigate issues pertaining to its fruitful implementation.

---

[33] Oakham, "Formation of Uncatechized Christians," in *One at the Table*, 85.
[34] Joseph A. Favazza, "Reconciliation as Second Baptism," in *One at the Table*, 44.

Part II

The Birth of a Rite

Chapter 2

The Reception of Heretics

The two "parents" that gave birth to the new rite for the reception of baptized Christians were the historical development of the liturgical rite for receiving heretics and the contemporary ecumenical movement. The rite of reception evolved from the long history of receiving back into the fold those who were outside it—some by their own volition, others by birth. The new rite was refined through the dialogues of the ecumenical movement in the years before and during the Second Vatican Council.

> Three terms are key to understanding these developments: heresy, schism, and apostasy.
>
> Heresy is the obstinate denial or obstinate doubt after the reception of baptism of some truth which is to be believed by divine and Catholic faith; apostasy is the total repudiation of the Christian faith; schism is the refusal of submission to the Supreme Pontiff or of communion with the members of the Church subject to him,[1]

All three categories presume the person in question has been validly baptized but occupies a status outside "communion." In the Catholic view, baptism does not immediately admit one to communion.

It is sometimes difficult to distinguish heresy from schism because they both involve someone whose beliefs about life in Christ lie outside the communion of the Catholic Church. Noteworthy examples of schism include the Orthodox Churches. An early example of heresy was Arianism, which denied the divinity of Jesus Christ. An apostate, however, is someone who, after baptism, renounces Christianity altogether and pursues a non-Christian path—either a peaceful path

---

[1] CCL, 751.

to holiness such as Buddhism, or a violent path toward evil such as religious-based terrorism. In the early church, "apostate" could refer to a faithful Christian who crossed over to a heretical Christian sect. Today the term is reserved for one who has abandoned Christianity altogether.

The landscape of Christian beliefs has been altered considerably since the early church, but a review of the history of receiving heretics will help explain why the late-twentieth-century Rite of Reception of Baptized Christians into the Full Communion of the Catholic Church differs so much from its antecedents.[2]

THE BAPTISM OF HERETICS

The early church first had to deal with this practical question about heretics who desired to return to the fold: "Should they be baptized?" For example, if one born to a Nestorian family underwent baptism in that unorthodox sect and then desired to renounce Nestorian belief and join orthodox Christianity, should that person be (re-)baptized? Eventually, the church said no, overriding the voices of those, such as Tertullian, who answered yes. The first of the Latin fathers of the church, Tertullian wrote from North Africa around the turn of the third century. He believed that the baptism of heretics was invalid, and that those coming to the orthodox Christian faith from heresies should be baptized:

> Heretics do not share our way of life. . . . They and we do not have one and the same God, nor one and the same Christ. Therefore we do not have one and the same baptism either. . . . They cannot undergo baptism because they do not have it.[3]

[2] This chapter relies heavily on the invaluable research performed by Dale J. Sieverding for the Pontifical Liturgical Institute, Sant' Anselmo, and published in his dissertation, Ordo admissionis valide iam baptizatorum in plenam communionem ecclesiae catholicae: *An Historical Study of the Ritual Aspects of Reception into Full Communion with Special Attention to the Adaptations of the Rite for Use in the Catholic Church in the United States* (Rome: 1997). This work was abridged in a more accessible publication in the Forum Essays series, *The Reception of Baptized Christians: A History and Evaluation* (Chicago: Liturgy Training Publications, 2001). The author acknowledges his debt to Sieverding's work.

[3] Tertullian, *De baptismo* 15:2, CCL 1:290. Translations are the author's unless otherwise noted.

We receive heretics just like Gentiles—indeed, as even more than Gentiles. People are removed from either category through a real baptism.[4]

In third-century Rome, though, opinions were split. According to Hippolytus, Pope Callistus took a lax view toward reconciling heretics: "Let the tares grow along with the wheat" (Matt 13:30).[5] Hippolytus desired more concrete penitential actions. This dispute is recorded only in the work of Hippolytus; history has not preserved any pertinent writing of Callistus.

The two sides were more sharply drawn in the next generation. Cyprian of Carthage restated the rigorist position of Tertullian: "Those who do not have the Holy Spirit cannot baptize at all."[6] This laid the groundwork for the baptism of heretics coming to orthodox Christianity:

> If from the heretics comes someone who was not first baptized in the church, but comes as a complete outsider and a pagan, he or she must be baptized in order to become a sheep, because there is only one water that makes sheep in the holy church.[7]

But some were first legitimately baptized, migrated to heresy, and then wanted to return to the fold. For these apostates, Cyprian advocated handlaying, not baptism. This less controversial opinion influenced later developments:

> It is enough to impose the hand in penitence upon those who had been baptized here and crossed over from us to become heretics, if they later return to the truth and to the womb, having acknowledged their sin and cast off error.[8]

Pope Stephen, a contemporary of Cyprian, differed on the issue of heretic baptisms. None of Stephen's writings has survived. His position is largely known through the letters of Cyprian, who opposed

---

[4] Tertullian, *De pudicitia* 19:5, CCL 2:1320.

[5] Hippolytus, *Refutatio omnium haeresium* 9:12, 22; *Patristiche Texte und Studien* 25 (Berlin/New York: 1986) 355.

[6] Cyprian, *Epistula* 69:10, Corpus scriptorum ecclesiasticorum latinorum [CSEL] 3/2:759.

[7] Cyprian, *Epistula* 71:2, CSEL 3/2:773.

[8] Cyprian, *Epistula* 71:2, CSEL 3/2:772–73.

him. Stephen affirmed the validity of the baptism of heretics, and he admitted to communion those who desired it. He observed that the heretics received one another in this way. But to Cyprian it was absurd for the Orthodox Church to follow the procedures of heretics and to say that the Holy Spirit was conferred in their baptism but not in their handlaying:

> If [heretics] attribute the effectiveness of baptism to the majesty of the name, so that those who are baptized wherever and however in the name of Jesus Christ are considered renewed and sanctified, by what internal logic is the hand also imposed on the baptized in the name of the same Christ, for them to receive the Holy Spirit? Why does not the same majesty of the same name, which they contend was valid in the sanctification of baptism, have such power in [their] handlaying?[9]

In a letter from Firmilianus, bishop of Caesarea, to Cyprian, the author summarizes Stephen's position in a similar way:

> Stephen says that the name of Christ for the most part leads to faith and to the sanctification of baptism, so that anyone who has been baptized anywhere in the name of Christ at once obtains the grace of Christ.[10]

In one of history's ironies, Callistus and Stephen prevailed, even though none of their original work on this topic has survived. Their positions are known only through the filters of their opponents Hippolytus and Cyprian. Perhaps they won out because they were bishops of Rome. Or perhaps it was because Augustine threw the considerable weight of his influential support behind their thinking.

At the turn of the fifth century Augustine wrote that Christ was the ultimate minister of baptism, and that "when the water of baptism is given to anyone in the name of the Father, the Son and the Holy Spirit, it is neither ours nor yours."[11] He distinguished between the administration of baptism and the power of the sacrament. An unworthy minister could still be the instrument of God's power, because it is Christ who baptizes. Commenting on the opening chapter of Paul's

---

[9] Cyprian, *Epistula* 74:5, CSEL 3/2:802–3.
[10] Cyprian, *Epistula* 75:18, CSEL 3/2:822.
[11] Augustine, *Contra litteras Petiliani* 2:2,5, CSEL 52:24.

First Letter to the Corinthians, where the church was splintering into factions according to the minister of baptism, Augustine says,

> Paul baptized as a minister, not as power itself. But the Lord baptized as power. . . . The Lord kept to himself the power of baptizing; he gave its administration to his servants.[12]

Augustine even reinterpreted the teaching of Cyprian, who actually promoted the opposite position Augustine assigned him:

> We use blessed Cyprian as a witness that the ancient custom of the catholic church should be held now: when coming from among heretics or schismatics, if people have received baptism consecrated with the words of the gospel, they are not baptized again.[13]

"Should heretics be baptized?" This fundamental question was laid to rest early in church history. Those who took the rigorist position in favor of baptizing heretics lost to the contrary opinion. The early church believed that the baptism of heretics was valid, and the later church never changed this view.

During the third and fourth centuries, then, some former heretics were joining the group that was coming to be known as orthodox Christianity or the Catholic Church. Some ritual needed to happen to mark this transition. They were already validly baptized. They would have to be received in some other way.

RECEPTION BY HANDLAYING

The primary method for receiving heretics became handlaying. Augustine, who rejected the suitableness of baptism in these cases, explained:

> A hand is imposed on reformed heretics because of the union of charity, which is the greatest gift of the Holy Spirit, and without which any other holy things that are in a person have no power for salvation.[14]

At first there was not one single method for reception. A late-fourth-century council in Laodicea in Phrygia did not explicitly mention

[12] Augustine, *In Iohannis Evangelium Tractatus* 5:7, CCL 36:44.
[13] Augustine, *De baptismo* 5:1,1, CSEL 51:261.
[14] Augustine, *De baptismo* 5:24,33, CSEL 51:290.

handlaying, but it introduced two other elements for the reception of those returning from heresies—they were to renounce all heresies, undergo catechesis on the creed, and be anointed with chrism:

> Concerning those who return from heresies—Novatians, Photinians, or Quartodecimans—whether catechumens or faithful in these sects, let them not be received before having renounced all heresies, and in particular those they have left. Those among them who are called faithful in these sects may participate in the holy mystery after having learned the creed of the faith and having been anointed with holy chrism.[15]

A contemporaneous ecumenical council in Constantinople called for the same components—renunciation and anointing—along with a spoken formula. Once again, handlaying was not explicitly mentioned. The anointing of several parts of the face is unusual:

> Those who embrace orthodoxy and join the number of those who are being saved from heretics . . . we receive when they hand in statements and anathematise every heresy which is not of the same mind as the holy, catholic and apostolic church of God. They are first sealed or anointed with holy chrism on the forehead, eyes, nostrils, mouth and ears. As we seal them we say: "Seal of the gift of the holy Spirit."[16]

Among the popes, Siricius handed on a tradition he had received that heretics join the company of Catholics "only through the invocation of the sevenfold Spirit by the imposition of a bishop's hand."[17] In this case, he mentioned both the gesture—handlaying—and a prayer for the coming of the Holy Spirit with seven gifts. A prayer for seven gifts of the Spirit first appeared in the baptismal liturgy of Ambrose.[18] The prayer was inspired by the list of spiritual gifts for an anointed king in Isaiah 11.

---

[15] Hefele-Leclercq, *Histoire des conciles*, 1.2, 999. Translation from the French by Turner, *Sources of Confirmation from the Fathers Through the Reformers* (Collegeville: Liturgical Press, 1993) 88.

[16] *Decrees of the Ecumenical Councils*, ed. Norman P. Tanner (Washington DC: Georgetown University Press, 1990) 35.

[17] Siricius, *Epistula* 1:2, Patrologia Latina [PL] 13:1133.

[18] Ambrose, *De mysteriis* 7:42, *Sources Chrétiennes* 25bis:178.

Pope Innocent I distinguished the purposes of two methods. In an early-fifth-century letter, he called for handlaying on those joining the church from heresies, but penance for returning apostates:

> Those coming from the Novatians or the Montanists may be received by the imposition of the hand only, because they were indeed baptized in the name of Christ, although by heretics. This does not apply to those who were allegedly baptized again when they crossed over from us to them. If these wish to return—coming to their senses and realizing their perdition—they must be admitted under a long satisfaction of penance.[19]

But the distinctions were not clean. To Innocent, handlaying on retuning heretics itself signified penitence—as it had to Cyprian—as well as sanctification in the Holy Spirit. He believed the baptism of heretics was valid, but that it somehow lacked the Holy Spirit:

> Moreover, we receive Arians—and other such pests whose laity have converted to the Lord—through handlaying, under the sign of penitence and sanctification of the Holy Spirit. . . . We concede that their one baptism is approved because it is indeed done in the name of the Father, the Son and the Holy Spirit, but we judge that they do not have the Holy Spirit from that baptism and those mysteries.[20]

Innocent did not mention the practices of renouncing heresies or anointing with chrism. The tradition was not yet uniform.

Leo the Great, who served as pope several decades after Innocent, also distinguished heretics from apostates. Some members of the faithful—apostates—had accepted baptism by heretics but were wishing to return to the fold. Leo prescribed "that they do not receive the unity of communion in our community except through the remedy of penance and the imposition of the bishop's hand."[21]

Others had been baptized for the first time among the heretics and wished to join the Catholic Church. Leo continued to forbid the practice of baptizing them. Instead, he said,

[19] Innocent I, *Epistula* 2:8, 11 PL 20:475.
[20] Innocent I, *Epistula* 24, 4 PL 20:549–50.
[21] Leo the Great, *Epistula* 159:6, PL 54:1138.

They must be confirmed only by the invocation of the Holy Spirit through the imposition of hands because they received only the form of baptism without the power of sanctification. . . . Only the sanctification of the Holy Spirit must be invoked. In this way, that which no one receives from heretics is obtained from catholic bishops.[22]

For Leo, apostates returned to the fold through penance and hand-laying. But heretics who had never been part of the fold were joined to it through handlaying—not baptism and not penance—through which they received the power of the Holy Spirit lacking in their baptism. Their baptism was considered valid, and penance was not necessary because they had not made a conscious decision to leave orthodox Christianity—they had started out in a heretical sect.

Leo used the term "confirmed" in this passage, but it is too early in the history of the sacrament of confirmation to assume that Leo meant the same thing. Some members of the faithful, having been baptized by a priest or a deacon, later celebrated confirmation with the bishop. Here the word seems to have a juridical sense indicating that their heretical condition was now regularized.

By the time of Gregory the Great (590–604), the reception of heretics "to the womb of mother church" was being done in several ways:

either by the anointing of chrism, handlaying, or a mere profession of faith. For this reason, the West restores Arians to the door of the Catholic Church through handlaying, but the East through the anointing of sacred chrism. But the Church receives Monophysites and others by a simple true profession of faith.[23]

All these texts speak of "receiving" "reformed" heretics who are "coming" or "returning." They do not speak of "forgiving" heretics or having them do "penance."[24] The language of penitence was reserved to apostates—members of the faithful who ventured into heresy but then returned, contrite, to the catholic fold.

Even at this level of discourse among popes, bishops, councils, and theologians, one senses not only a global yearning for unity but also the inner personal turmoil of individuals. Many people had struggled

[22] Ibid., 7, PL 54:1138–39.
[23] Gregory the Great, *Liber* 11, *Epistula* 52, CCL 140A:952–53.
[24] Except for Innocent I, *Epistula* 24.

with their faith, God, family, friends, authorities, triumphs, and sorrows. They were regarded by the Catholic Church as heretics or even pests. But after prayerful consideration, they still sought union with its company.

Ritual texts have not survived from these centuries. It is unknown beyond these sketchy references how the liturgies in question proceeded. Bishops are mentioned as the ministers because they were also the ordinary ministers of baptism at the time, because writings of the period tell more of bishops than of other ministers and laity, and because many bishops of the time governed areas no more populous than those overseen by pastors in large parishes today.

This much seems clear: Those who began their Christian life in a heretical sect and who wished to join the Catholic fold were not to be baptized again; instead, the bishop performed one or more, but probably not all, of these actions: He asked for a renunciation of heresies, heard a profession of faith, imposed hands, anointed with chrism, and/or prayed for the coming of the Spirit. The point was to ritualize the conferral of the Holy Spirit on those whose baptisms were officially valid but spiritually shallow. The practice distinguished two types of baptized Christians—those who were orthodox and those were not.

MEDIEVAL LITURGICAL TEXTS

By the eighth century the liturgy of the church became more unified through the compilation and sharing of liturgical texts in books of orders, sacramentaries, and pontificals. Editors codified an oral tradition of prayers and rubrics. Copyists wittingly increased the number of books—and unwittingly increased the variations within them. The medieval liturgical books fed the swelling river of uniformity in the church's worship. The rituals for receiving heretics formed one eddy in the current.

The first examples of prayer texts for the reception of heretics come from the Gelasian Sacramentary. Originally composed in seventh-century Rome for use by priests in local churches, this book was carried to Gaul where it underwent revisions. The oldest extant copy of the Gelasian comes from Chelles near Paris, about the year 750. But many of its texts are probably Roman, dating from a century or two earlier.

Witnesses from the early church stated that prayers were said over returning heretics. The Gelasian contains the first recorded examples of them. Their appearance in a book designed for use by priests makes it plausible that bishops were sharing the ministry of reception. The examples open with this one:

A blessing over those who return to Catholic unity from Arianism

Lord God almighty, Father of our Lord Jesus Christ,
you who were pleased to rescue your male and female servants
from the error and lie of the Arian heresy
and to guide them to your catholic Church,
send onto them, Lord, the holy paraclete,
the spirit of wisdom and understanding, the spirit of counsel and
 fortitude,
the spirit of knowledge and piety,
and fill them, Lord, with the spirit of the fear of God,
in the name of Jesus Christ, our saving God,
through whom and with whom all honor and glory is yours for
 ever and ever.
Amen.[25]

No rubrics appear with this text. Its title calls it a "blessing," and it invokes the sevenfold Holy Spirit. It would be logical to conclude that the priest or bishop saying this prayer imposed one or both hands over those returning, either touching the heads of individuals or extending hands over a group. After all, as early as the fourth century Siricius had instructed bishops to receive heretics with handlaying and a prayer enumerating these gifts. He was passing on a tradition he had already received, presumably from the writings of Ambrose, who had included the gifts of the Spirit in his commentary on the baptismal liturgy. It is possible that the tradition of handlaying continued as an accompaniment to this eighth-century prayer.

The prayer does not indicate an anointing. The text is intent less on rubrics and more on explicit references to the heresy left behind, Arianism, which denied the divinity of Christ. The closing of this prayer significantly identifies him as "our saving God" (*dei salvatoris nostri*).

The Gelasian next includes this prayer as an alternative:

[25] *Liber sacramentorum Romane aeclesiae ordinis anni circuli (Sacramentarium Gelasianum)*, ed. Leo Cunibert Mohlberg (Rome: Casa Editrice Herder, 1981) 683. Hereafter, GeV.

Another one for those who come from other heresies

Holy Father, almighty God,
you who were pleased to rescue your servant
from the error of heresies,
and to call him (her) to the holy catholic Church,
we ask you, Lord, send onto him (her) the paraclete, your holy
    sevenfold Spirit,
the spirit of wisdom and understanding, of counsel and fortitude,
of knowledge and piety;
pour into your servant the spirit of the fear of God,
through our Lord Jesus Christ.[26]

This prayer is similar to the first, though it omits the explicit references to Arianism. Like the first, it has no rubrics; but because of the nature of the prayer and its title (*Item*—"another one") referring to the word "blessing" in the first prayer, it is reasonable to assume it was accompanied with handlaying. The action of God is described as "calling" (*advocare*) in this prayer, whereas it was "guiding" (*perducere*) in the first. These verbs describe the act of reception. These individual heretics are not coming "back" to the church but approaching it for the first time under the hand of God.

The other three prayers from this section are for apostates, those who began life within the Catholic community, were baptized again by heretics, and desired to return. These are grouped under the heading, "Reconciliation of Someone Baptized Again by Heretics." Their tone is more penitential, for example, "May he (she) worthily complete the fruit of penance by your mercy." These are the individuals who needed "reconciliation" with the church.[27]

The Gelasian Sacramentary underwent further revisions. The compilation known as the Gellone Sacramentary probably dates to the end of the eighth century. The second of the old Gelasian prayers is virtually repeated. But the first underwent two noteworthy changes. It received a new title: "The Reconciliation of Those Returning from the Pagans." And it included this ending:

Fill him (her), Lord, with the Spirit of fear of you, so that in the name of our Lord Jesus Christ, he (she) may be signed with the

[26] GeV 684.
[27] GeV 685–86.

sign of the cross in eternal life. Through the same Jesus Christ our
Lord, your Son, who lives and reigns with you forever as God,
one with the Holy Spirit.[28]

The meaning of these changes is not clear. Perhaps, in the specific
time and place where this copy of the Sacramentary was made, there
were no Arians; but there may have been apostates who had drifted
from the Christian fold and were seeking to return. This would
explain the introduction of the words "reconciliation" and "returning"
to the title of the prayer. The full text, however, still uses the word
"guide" (*perducere*), and it introduces no reference to reconciliation,
penitence, or forgiveness. It does include an explicit sign of the cross.
One possibility is that the text of the prayer evolved to indicate a
rubric thought to be fitting for the *reception* of heretics (not the reconciliation of apostates), and that the editor assigned a different *title* to
this prayer to satisfy the local need for a specific oration. Another possibility is that it is what it says: a prayer for reconciling apostates that
amplified the rubrics while de-emphasizing repentance. In either case,
the church was beginning to blur the distinction between heretics and
apostates.

A disjuncture between the title and the prayer appears in another
text from this group in the Gellone Sacramentary: the original text
prayed for returning apostates who had been baptized by heretics.[29]
The revised text in the Gellone inserts the word *absolvat*, indicating the
desire that God forgive the one returning. But the text bears the curious
title, "Prayer over Those who Eat Dead Things."[30] It strengthens the
possibility that the editor of the Gellone needed texts for some local
matters.

These examples have given no clear indication of rubrics that
accompanied the prayers. Further, they exist only as orations, completely isolated from any ritual. A complete ritual must have taken
place, but only prayers like these were recorded.

The first complete rite appears in the *Liber ordinum*. The earliest
extant manuscript of this Visigothic (Mozarabic) work comes from
the eleventh century, but its texts are judged to be considerably older.

---

[28] *Liber sacramentorvm Gellonensis*, Corpus Christianorum, Series Latina [CCL]
159:2396. Hereafter, GeG.

[29] GeV 687.

[30] GeG 2395.

The rites are called "reconciliations." The first begins with a formal renunciation of heresy and profession of faith.

> *First [the bishop] asks [the one returning] his (her) name and says to him (her):*
>
>> Do you renounce the heresy of the Arians, in which up to now you have regretfully been a member?
>
> **I renounce it.**
>
> Do you renounce those who say that the Son of God is less than the Father?
>
> **I renounce them.**
>
>> Do you renounce those who believe that the Holy Spirit is not God, or say the Spirit is less than the Father or the Son?
>
> **I renounce them.**
>
> *Again he asks his (her) name, and says to him (her):*
>
> N., do you believe in God the Father almighty?
>
> **I believe.**
>
> Do you believe in Jesus Christ his Son?
>
> **I believe.**
>
>> Do you believe in the Holy Spirit, in a God of undivided Trinity, essential unity, strength and power?
>
> **I believe.**
>
>> After this profession of faith, the bishop anoints the one returning, while saying this text:
>>
>> I chrismate you in the name of the Father, and of the Son, and of the Holy Spirit, in forgiveness of all your sins, that you may have eternal life. Amen.
>
> *After this, he lays a hand on him (her) and says the prayer of confirmation.*

This lengthy prayer includes a petition that the one returning may persevere in the Holy Spirit:

> Turn your gaze upon this your servant, we pray, whom we present to you in sincerity, offering a living victim, who has now converted to you, who, wandering from the truth for a while, has finally set foot in your flock. The one about to enter to you—indeed, through

you—about to remain from now on in your church, deserves its communion, hurrying to his (her) mother church, in which no heresy, no perversity, no division and no impiety remains, but true and lasting peace, which divine grace has established and the doctrine of the apostles has made firm, and holy faith has obtained.

Give him (her) therefore, Lord, the spirit of wisdom and understanding, the spirit of counsel and fortitude, the spirit of knowledge and piety, and confirm in him (her) the spirit of divine fear, so that, joined to your faithful people and gathered into the flock with your chosen ones, he (she) may obey your will, and no one may grasp him (her) from your hand, but may he (she) persevere in the true and catholic faith, to which he (she) comes under your inspiration, and in which he (she) lives under your protection for ever.[31]

This text is ambiguous enough to cover the circumstance of both apostates and heretics. The title is "reconciliation," which is the language of one returning from apostasy. The unique formula of chrismation explicitly calls for the "forgiveness of all your sins," indicating that this anointing served as the bridge of forgiveness leading toward the gift of the sevenfold Spirit. Furthermore, the prayer speaks of one who was "wandering from the truth for a while," who will "remain from now on in your church," which would also signify an apostate returning to the fold.

But the same text embellishes the prayer for the sevenfold Spirit with the petition that the person be "joined to your faithful people and gathered into the flock," as if this had not been the case before. It may be that the distinction between heresy and apostasy was not sharp, and the same prayers were used for those entering the church from Arianism, whether or not they began life faithful in the church. If so, the medieval church presumed that heretics were sinners who should repent, a position that differed from that of the early church.

The *Liber ordinvm* used the word "confirmation" for this prayer and the handlaying that accompanied it. By this time the word "confirmation" was coming to mean a ceremony separate from baptism, in which bishops conferred the Holy Spirit upon those who had earlier

---

[31] *Le* Liber Ordinvm *en usage dan l'église wisigothique et mozarabe d'espagne du cinquième au onzième siècle*, Monvmenta Ecclesiae Litvrgica 5:100–103 (Paris: Librairie de Firmin-Didot et Cie, 1904).

been baptized. The church had not yet defined the dogmas that there are seven sacraments and that confirmation could not be repeated. In short, the term "confirmation" still lacked some precision. It may well be that this prayer in the *Liber ordinvm* is referring to someone baptized in orthodox Christianity, who had been confirmed, became an apostate, and was reconciled to the fold through an anointing and prayer for the sevenfold gift of the Spirit. But such a ritual would not have been regarded then as confirmation is regarded now.

In the *Liber ordinvm* this complete liturgy of reconciliation is followed by two orations—one for returning apostates and another for reformed Donatists. They are probably appended as alternates for the first part of the "prayer of confirmation" in the complete liturgy. The presence of these orations might indicate that the first prayer was also for apostates, forming a complete group, or that it was not, and alternatives were needed.[32]

Another Spanish sacramentary from the eleventh century includes a complete liturgy. This original rite appears in the *Sacramentarium Rivipullense* under the title "Order for Reconciling an Apostate Converted from Judaism, Heresy, or Paganism." It is not clear whether this was intended for a true apostate, in the sense of one individual who began life as a faithful Christian, or if the term at this time and place more broadly applied to the group of those outside Christianity. It seems that the terms "heretic" and "apostate" had become interchangeable.

The order includes an exorcism, entrance into the church, prostration by the convert while penitential psalms were prayed, two prayers for the reconciling of apostates taken from the Gellone, a renunciation of Satan, consignation with chrism, penance, and communion.[33]

The *Rivipullense* was not well known, but William Durandus, bishop of Mende, had access to it. And his pontifical became one of the most influential liturgical books in the Middle Ages. The thirteenth-century pontifical of Durandus collected and created rituals needed by bishops. His "Order for Reconciling Apostates, Schismatics or Heretics" guided a bishop through a complete liturgy for accepting validly baptized

---

[32] *Liber Ordinvm* 103–5.

[33] *Sacramentarium Rivipullense*, Monumenta Hispaniae sacra, Series liturgica 7:1422–1429, Madris-Barcelona 1964.

candidates into the fold of the Catholic Church. It was the most thorough and widely used liturgy of this kind to survive.[34]

The title of this order brings to a head the theological development of these medieval liturgical books. The differences among apostates, schismatics, and heretics were deemed so slight that all could be treated by the same liturgical text. Apostates received no special treatment—but neither did schismatics and heretics. In fact, the liturgical language in use for returning apostates was now applied in every case to the reception of schismatics and heretics as well. Whereas in the patristic era apostates only were "called back to the Church," "reconciled," and "forgiven," Durandus applied these terms to heretics and schismatics. By inference, they were being charged with the same sin as apostates. It did not matter that they were born into a heretical sect. Their reception into the church was termed "reconciliation."

The rite began outside. At the time, this is how the order for becoming a catechumen began. Those who were unbaptized were greeted at the door of the church and exorcized before entering the building and beginning their formation.[35] Durandus chose the same symbol for this rite:

> The reconciliation of an apostate happens in this way. First, outside the doors of the church, the bishop or priest asks him (or her) about his (her) faith.[36]

Then the bishop offers a prayer of exorcism. In the rite for becoming a catechumen, this prayer assumed the devil had free reign over one who had never been part of the Body of Christ. Here the exorcism assumes the devil could also influence a member who was already validly baptized. It begins with these words:

---

[34] Michel Andrieu, *Le Pontifical Romain au Moyen-âge, Le Pontifical de Guillaume Durand* (Vatican City: Biblioteca Apostolica Vaticana, 1940) 3:9, 616–19.

[35] Michel Andrieu, *Le Pontifical Romain au Moyen-âge, Le Pontifical Romain de la Curie Romaine au XIIIe Siècle* (Vatican City: Biblioteca Apostolica Vaticana, 1940) 2:53, 513.

[36] The pontifical says "bishop or priest" here. But the entire book was written for the ceremonies over which bishops presided. It is possible that priests celebrated this rite on occasion, as they presumably did with the Gelasian texts, but it is unlikely because of the inclusion of the prayer for the sevenfold Spirit, so closely associated at this time with the sacrament of confirmation. It may also be that a priest assisting the bishop was permitted to begin the liturgy with the question. Or, it could have been an editor's oversight.

> I exorcize you, unclean spirit, through God the almighty Father and through Jesus Christ his Son and the Holy Spirit, that you may leave this servant of God, whom God and our Lord is pleased to free from your errors and lies, and to call back to the holy, catholic and apostolic mother Church.[37]

The text expresses the belief that God is calling this person back—even though he or she may personally never have been part of the orthodox faith. The person is then signed with the cross.

> Then he signs him (her) with the sign of the cross, saying, "Receive + the sign of the cross of Christ and of Christianity, which, having once received, you did not keep, but having been deceived by evil, you denied."[38]

The text assumes the person received a valid baptism and apostatized, even if he or she never personally did.

> Then he brings him (her) into the church, saying, "Enter the church of God, from which you carelessly wandered, and realize that you have escaped the snares of death. Abhor idols; repudiate every heretical, pagan or Jewish distortion or superstition. Worship the almighty God and Jesus Christ his Son and the Holy Spirit, the living and true God, the holy and undivided Trinity. And you, almighty God, in paternal compassion, take (*percipe*) this your lamb, extracted from the jaws of the wolf by your might, and in your kindness set him (her) again (*refirma*) in your flock, so that the enemy may not rejoice in the damnation of your family, but that the devoted mother of the restored son (daughter) may be thankful for his (her) conversion and liberation in your church. Through Christ our Lord."[39]

In this prayer Durandus continues the language formerly reserved for apostates. Individuals had "carelessly wandered," God was taking them and setting them again in the flock, and mother church rejoices in the restoration of a child nearly lost. No changes were made to this prayer for converts from Judaism or non-Christian religions.

---

[37] Andrieu 3:9 (2), 616.
[38] Andrieu 3:9 (3), 616.
[39] Andrieu 3:9 (4), 616–17.

Inside the church, probably once all have taken their places, a prayer lifted from the Gelasian tradition was made. It asks God to

> look kindly upon this your servant, that what was stolen away by hostile force and diabolical fraud due to his (her) inattention (*ignorantie*), the indulgence of your compassion may excuse and absolve, so that after the communion of your truth has been received, he (she) may be restored (*reddatur*) to the sacred altar. Through Christ our Lord.[40]

The one being reconciled then answers affirmatively to questions about his or her belief in the principal tenets of the creed. The format is traditional: "Do you believe in God?" "I believe." And so forth. Interestingly, the renunciation of Satan *follows* this profession of faith. The liturgy presumes that the one being reconciled holds a Christian faith, and the issue now is to abjure heresy:

> Sir (Madam), do you renounce Satan and his angels?
>
> **I renounce them.**
>
> Do you renounce his deeds and domains?
>
> **I renounce them.**
>
>> Do you also renounce every pagan sect, heretical distortion, or Jewish superstition?
>
> **I renounce them.**
>
> Do you wish to be and to live in the unity of the holy Catholic faith?
>
> **I wish it.**[41]

That final question is a variation on one in the baptismal rite, "Do you wish to be baptized?"[42] The bishop then imposes a hand on the head of the one being reconciled and says this prayer:

> Lord God almighty, Father of our Lord Jesus Christ, you who were pleased kindly to rescue this your servant from

[40] Andrieu 3:9 (5), 617.

[41] Andrieu 3:9 (7), 617.

[42] Michel Andrieu, *Le Pontifical Romain du XIIᵉ Siècle* (Vatican City: Biblioteca Apostolica Vaticana, 1938) 1:32, 24.

the error of pagans, the lie of distorted heresy, or of the superstition of Judaism, and to call him (her) back to your church, send, Lord, on him (her) the Holy Spirit, the Paraclete, from heaven. Resp. **Amen.**

The Spirit of wisdom and understanding. Resp. **Amen.**

The Spirit of counsel and fortitude. Resp. **Amen.**

The Spirit of knowledge and piety. Resp. **Amen.**

Fill him (her) with the spirit of the fear of the Lord, so that he (she) may be signed for eternal life with the sign + of the cross, in the name of our Lord Jesus Christ. Resp. **Amen.**[43]

No anointing is mentioned, probably because Durandus assumed that the one being reconciled had already been anointed once, and he wanted to avoid confusion between this ritual and confirmation. Still, this prayer for the sevenfold Spirit is based on one from the confirmation rite, and the bishop imposes a hand on the one being reconciled. But in confirmation, the bishop said explicitly, "I sign you with the sign of the cross, and I confirm you with the chrism of salvation. In the name + of the Father and + of the Son and of the Holy + Spirit, that you may be filled with the same Holy Spirit and have eternal life."[44] It appears that the meaning of the handlaying had more to do with reconciliation than with confirmation.

It is possible that Durandus meant for the bishop to read certain parts of the text with one of three options. For example, he might have intended this prayer to mention pagans, heresy, or Judaism, but not all three. Most likely, though, a bishop who wanted a pontifical in front of him would read all the words on the page.

Durandus includes two more prayers—one for the return of a person who originated a schism or who was well known as the promoter of one, and another for the originator or promoter of heresy. This person would read a more elaborate profession of faith and abjuration of false beliefs.

Throughout the Middle Ages, liturgical books developed a rite for those being received from heresies, and the distinction between heretics and apostates was lost. For the first time in history, returning heretics were reconciled, not received.

---

[43] Andrieu, *Le Pontifical de Guillaume Durand* 3:9 (8) 617–18.
[44] Andrieu 3:1 (3) 334.

The reconciliation of heretics underwent another adjustment after the Council of Trent, which convened in the sixteenth century to counter the Protestant Reformation. Christianity became mired in a contentious bog of zealots hurling mutual accusations of schisms and heresies. This period was characterized more by the dividing of Christianity than the reconciliation of its factions. The climate bore some similarities to circumstances in the early church, when dearly held beliefs were challenged, and theologians rose to the task of clarifying them. Eventually the sides had to deal with the question of how to receive someone crossing over. The Catholic Church began its response with the Council of Trent.

Two of the canons restated noncontroversial beliefs pertinent to this discussion. Baptism, validly conferred, was valid, and it was not to be repeated when someone was converted:

> If anyone says that baptism, which is also given by the heretics in the name of the Father, the Son and the Holy Spirit, with the intention of doing what the church does, is not true baptism, let him (her) be anathema.
>
> If anyone says that a true and rightly conferred baptism must be repeated for a person who denied the faith of Christ among infidels, but then is converted to penitence, let him (her) be anathema.[45]

After the council, two liturgical books explained what to do when a baptized Christian wanted to become Catholic: the pontifical of 1595, and the Roman Ritual of 1614.

The "Order for Reconciling an Apostate, Schismatic or Heretic" in the 1595 pontifical is almost the same as the one created by Durandus. It added to the beginning of the ritual twelve questions from the tenets of the creed.[46] The bishop led the one being reconciled by the hand into the church building, where he offered prayers.[47] The bishop then

---

[45] Canons 4 and 11, *Enchiridion Symbolorum*, ed. Henricus Denzinger and Adolfus Schonmetzer, 860, 867.

[46] *Pontificale Romanum*, Editio Princeps (1595–1596), ed. Manlio Sodi – Achille Maria Triacca, Monumenta Liturgica Concilii Tridentini (Vatican City: Libreria Editrice Vaticana, 1997) 648–49.

[47] Ibid., 650.

laid his right hand on the person's head.[48] The final clause of the prayer for the sevenfold Spirit changed from "fill him (her) with the Spirit of fear of the Lord" to "fill him (her) with the light of your splendor." Even these changes were minor. It is substantially the ritual of Durandus.

However, the Roman Ritual of 1614 introduced some theoretical clarifications.

This ritual collected the noneucharistic liturgical celebrations of the church in a handy volume, and the rites were revised to assist the driving force of the Counter-Reformation. The introduction to the rite of baptism, for example, makes these points:

> After the matter has been diligently investigated, all those for whom there is a probable doubt concerning their baptism, if nothing else impedes it, should be baptized conditionally.
> Heretics, though, coming to the Catholic Church, in whose baptism the proper form or matter was not preserved, must be baptized correctly; but first, they should acknowledge and detest the distortion of their errors, and be diligently instructed in the Catholic faith; however, whenever the proper form and matter was preserved, only the omitted rites should be supplied, unless the bishop deems otherwise for a reasonable cause.[49]

This seems logical enough. However, the *baptismal* liturgy expanded to include a renunciation of false worship. Previously, a renunciation of Satan sufficed. Now, those desiring baptism were asked formally to reject the system of belief to which they formerly adhered. Converts from paganism, Judaism, Islam, and Protestantism were all treated alike:

> *If the catechumen comes from the error of the Gentiles, or from paganism or idolaters, the priest says,*

Abhor idols. Reject effigies.

> *If he (she) comes from the Hebrews, he says,*

Abhor the Jewish perfidy. Reject the superstition of the Jews.

---

[48] Ibid., 651.

[49] *Rituale Romanum*, "De baptismo adultorum," 15–16 (Regensburg: Pustet, 1912) 22.

If he (she) comes from Islam, he says,

Abhor the Islamic perfidy. Reject the distorted sect of unfaithfulness.

> *If he (she) comes from the Heretics, and if the proper form was not observed in his (her) baptism, he says,*
>
> Abhor heretical distortion. Reject the nefarious sects of the impious (N.), *expressing by its proper name the sect from which he (she) comes.*
>
> Worship God the almighty Father and Jesus Christ, his only Son our Lord, who will come to judge the living and the dead, and the world by fire. Amen.[50]

The order of baptism also included a formula for use in conditional baptisms:

> *But if it may be credibly doubted that the elect had been baptized in another form, the priest says,* N., if you have not been baptized, I baptize you in the name of the Father and of the Son and of the Holy Spirit.[51]

In practice, priests baptized conditionally almost everyone who had been previously baptized in a church considered heretical.

In the case of a person coming from a heretical sect, the priest gave absolution to take away the impediment of excommunication. He also baptized conditionally, in case the previous baptism had not been valid. One or the other of these processes actually brought about the result of church membership.[52]

The 1614 rite of baptism also included a chapter on supplying the ceremonies omitted from a valid baptism. It is essentially the same as the baptismal rite, except it omits the baptism. All the renunciations are included—even those from paganism, Judaism, and Islam, in which no baptism happened.[53] In supplying omitted rites, the church took no chances, even to the point of absurdity. In practice, though, this rite was probably used rarely, in favor of conditional baptism.

---

[50] Ibid., 28.

[51] Ibid., 40.

[52] Cf. Adrian Fortescue and J. B. O'Connell, *The Ceremonies of the Roman Rite Described* (Westminster: London, Burns, Oates and Washburne Ltd., 1953) 389.

[53] *Rituale Romanum,* 43–44.

This situation continued for centuries and was clarified in an instruction from the Congregation of the Holy Office in 1859:

> In the conversion of heretics an inquiry must first be made into the validity of the baptism received in heresy. After a diligent examination has been thus accomplished, if it was conferred invalidly or not at all, they absolutely must be baptized. But if, when the investigation is over, a probable doubt about the validity of baptism remains, then it is repeated conditionally. Finally, if it is determined that it was valid, they must be received only with the abjuration or the profession of faith. Therefore a threefold method of proceeding is distinguished in reconciling heretics:
>
> 1. If baptism is conferred absolutely, neither abjuration nor absolution follows because the sacrament of rebirth washes away everything.
>
> 2. If baptism must be repeated conditionally, it must take place in this order:
>   a. the abjuration or profession of faith
>   b. conditional baptism
>   c. sacramental confession with conditional absolution.
>
> 3. Therefore, when baptism has been judged valid, only the abjuration or profession of faith is received, which is followed by the absolution from censures.[54]

The Holy Office gave these directions:

> The priest vested in alb and violet stole sits on the Epistle side of the altar (if the Blessed Sacrament is kept in the tabernacle)—otherwise in the middle of the altar—and the newly-converted kneels before him. Touching the book of the gospels with his (her) right hand, he (she) makes the profession of faith as it is given below. If he (she) does not know how to read, the priest reads the profession slowly for him (her), so that the convert may understand it and pronounce it after the priest word for word.[55]

The profession of faith was made in the vernacular language of the convert. This translation appears in the acts of the Second Council of Baltimore:

[54] Sacra Congregatio Sancti Officii, 20 July 1859, *Codicis Iuris Canonici Fontes*, (Vatican City: Typis Polyglottis Vaticanis, 1951) 4:226–27.
[55] Ibid., 227.

I, N.N., having before my eyes the holy Gospels, which I touch with my hand, and knowing that no one can be saved without that faith which the Holy Catholic Apostolic Roman Church holds, believes, and teaches, against which I grieve that I have greatly erred, inasmuch as I have held and believed doctrines opposed to her teaching.

I now, with grief and contrition for my past errors, profess that I believe the Holy Catholic Apostolic Roman Church to be the only and true Church established on earth by Jesus Christ, to which I submit myself with my whole heart. I believe all the articles that she proposes to my belief, and I reject and condemn all that she rejects and condemns, and I am ready to observe all that she commands me. And especially, I profess that I believe:

One only God in three divine Persons, distinct from, and equal to, each other—that is to say, the Father, the Son, and the Holy Ghost;

The Catholic doctrine of the Incarnation, Passion, Death, and Resurrection of our Lord Jesus Christ; and the personal union of the two Natures, the divine and the human; the divine Maternity of the most holy Mary, together with her most spotless Virginity;

The true, real, and substantial presence of the Body, together with the Soul and Divinity of our Lord Jesus Christ, in the most holy Sacrament of the Eucharist;

The seven Sacraments instituted by Jesus Christ for the salvation of mankind; that is to say, Baptism, Confirmation, Eucharist, Penance, Extreme Unction, Order, Matrimony;

Purgatory, the Resurrection of the dead, Everlasting life;

The Primacy, not only of honor, but also of jurisdiction of the Roman Pontiff, successor of St. Peter, Prince of the Apostles, Vicar of Jesus Christ;

The veneration of the Saints and of their images;

The authority of the Apostolic and Ecclesiastical Traditions, and of the Holy Scriptures, which we must interpret, and understand only in the sense which our holy mother the Catholic Church has held, and does hold;

And everything else, that has been defined, and declared by the sacred Canons, and by the General Councils, especially by the holy Council of Trent.

With a sincere heart, therefore, and with unfeigned faith, I detest and abjure every error, heresy, and sect opposed to the said Holy

Catholic and Apostolic Roman Church. So help me God, and these his holy Gospels, which I touch with my hand.[56]

Although the church continued to take a stand against the conditional baptism of those considered validly baptized, the case of Protestants was thought doubtful. A commentary on the Second Council of Baltimore classified Protestants among heretics whose questionable beliefs about baptism might lead to its careless administration. As a result, those being received into the Catholic Church were to be conditionally baptized:

> The doctrine of the sectaries on the efficacy and necessity of baptism, and the consequent carelessness of these men in its administration, is one of the grave reasons that should induce us to doubt the validity of this sacrament as conferred by heretics.[57]

The Counter-Reformation ushered the Catholic Church into a lengthy period that assigned the Reformers the status of heretics—an assignation that was not condign. Divisions of heresies in the early church arose from issues pertaining to the Creed, but the churches of the Reform and Counter-Reform all retained allegiance to those same creeds. The fragmentation of the church was serious in the sixteenth century, but different from that in the early church. Using the ritual language at hand caused the problems to deepen.

In the few centuries leading up to the Reformation, the rite for receiving heretics had undergone subtle but significant changes. It had become more penitential in nature, being assigned the title "reconciliation of heretics." It conflated the earlier distinctions between apostates and heretics, requiring all those outside the church—not just those who had individually turned away from Catholicism, but all those born into other beliefs—to be reconciled.

Consequently, when some Protestant Christians sought to become Catholic, the Catholic Church offered them a rite based on the one it had immediately inherited from the Middle Ages. The procedure was considered to be a reconciliation of heretics, a forgiveness of sins, a release from censures, and possibly a baptism to replace one invalidly

[56] *Concilii Plenarii Baltimorensis II., Acta et Decreta* (Baltimore, 1868) 292–93.
[57] S. Smith, *Notes on the Second Plenary Council of Baltimore* (New York: P. O'Shea, 1874) 190–91.

conferred. In practice, then, the Catholic Church made little distinction between those coming from non-Christian traditions and those from Christian traditions of the Reformation. In conditional baptism, the liturgy included the words, "If you have not been baptized, I baptize you . . .," but this small insertion would have been little noticed in the elaborate ceremony of baptism, and it revealed that the validity of Protestant baptisms was deemed suspect.

When canon law was codified in 1917, it made these distinctions, which summarized the Catholic Church's understanding of the landscape of religious belief:

> If one, after the reception of baptism, while retaining the name of Christian, pertinaciously denies or doubts about any of the truths which must be believed by an obligation of divine and Catholic faith, he is a heretic; if he gives up the Christian faith entirely, he is an apostate; finally, if he refuses submission to the Supreme Pontiff or rejects communion with the members of the Church subject to the latter, he is a schismatic.[58]

In practice, though, when it came to admitting members of these groups to communion, they effectively underwent the same ceremony. And it was not considered a reception. It was reconciliation.

[58] John A. Abbo and Jerome D. Hannan, *The Sacred Canons: A Concise Presentation of the Current Disciplinary Norms of the Church* (St. Louis, London: B. Herder Book Co., 1957) 2:562.

Chapter 3

The Ecumenical Movement

If one parent of the post–Vatican II rite of reception was the historical development of the liturgical rite , the other parent was the ecumenical movement of the twentieth century. As time went by, the Christian church of the West sought to heal its divisions. This caused the various sides to look at one another with new eyes. Accusations of heresy virtually disappeared, and the rite of reception was adjusted in accordance with these new understandings.

PRECONCILIAR ACTIVITY

A question about marriage signaled the need for more careful thinking on the part of the Catholic Church. The Catholic Church believes in the indissolubility of marriage. If a divorced person seeks to be married in the Catholic Church, the church investigates the validity of the earlier marriage. Because of the intricacies of church law on this point, one's baptismal status must be established to determine the appropriate method for trying marriage cases. For example, if a marriage between two nonbaptized persons ends in divorce, the Catholic Church accepts the nullity of the marriage through a simpler procedure than if one or both were validly baptized. If there was a tendency to doubt the baptism of converts to the Catholic Church, there was a tendency to accept the baptism of divorced Christians. The paradox can be explained by the church's caution in administering sacraments.

Due to the variety of Christian expressions in the United States, it was becoming important to know which baptisms were to be considered valid and which were not. In 1949 the bishops of the United States asked for a clarification from the Holy Office:

In judging marriage cases, if the necessary matter and form were maintained, should the baptism conferred in the sects of the Disciples of Christ, Presbyterians, Congregationalists, Baptists, and Methodists be presumed invalid because of a defect of the minister's required intention to do that which the church does or which Christ instituted, or should it be presumed valid, unless it is proven to the contrary in a particular case?

The Holy Office responded in favor of these baptisms. Normally, they were considered valid: "No to the first part. Yes to the second."[1] Although this resulted in a more demanding application of church law concerning the validity of marriage, it should also have resulted in a more lax application of church law concerning the abjuration of heresy and the conferral of conditional baptism. But it took time.

In 1959 the Vatican revised the traditional Good Friday prayer for the Jews. Up to this time, that prayer called the Jews "perfidious." But the word was dropped as part of the revision because the church accepted the point that Jews were not without faith.[2]

At the same time the rite of baptism changed. The renunciation of false worship was no longer required of adults being baptized, and Jewish converts no longer repudiated their "perfidious" and "super-stitious" religion.[3] It was no longer presumed that those being baptized had engaged in false worship.

On the eve of the Second Vatican Council, it was becoming clear that the church needed different categories to speak about other Christians. This position was articulated in 1958 by Joseph Ratzinger, then a young priest, the future head of the Congregation for the Doctrine of the Faith under Pope John Paul II, and the future Pope Benedict XVI. These remarks are taken from an essay he prepared for the Theological Congress of the Austrian Institute for Pastoral Work in Vienna:

> There is no appropriate category in Catholic thought for the phe-
> nomenon of Protestantism today (one could say the same of the
> relationship to the separated Churches of the East). It is obvious
> that the old category of "heresy" is no longer of any value. Heresy,

---

[1] Acta Apostolicae Sedis 41 (1949) 650. Hereafter, AAS.

[2] Sacred Congregation of Rites, "Variationes in missali et in rituali romano in precibus pro iudaeis," *Ephemerides Liturgicae* 74 (1960) 133.

[3] Ibid.

for scripture and the early church, includes the idea of a personal decision against the unity of the church, and heresy's characteristic is *pertinacia*, the obstinacy of him who persists in his own private way. This, however, cannot be regarded as an appropriate description of the spiritual situation of the Protestant Christian. In the course of a now centuries-old history, Protestantism has made an important contribution to the realization of Christian faith, fulfilling a positive function in the development of the Christian message and, above all, often giving rise to a sincere and profound faith in the individual non-Catholic Christian, whose separation from the Catholic affirmation has nothing to do with the *pertinacia* characteristic of heresy. . . . We must try to think our way forward here in the spirit of the New Testament and to apply this spirit to all the things that did not exist then, but are in our world today.[4]

THE SECOND VATICAN COUNCIL

In 1959 Pope John XXIII announced the Second Vatican Council and opened its agenda to suggestions from the bishops of the world. Several wanted clarification on the validity of Protestant baptism. For example, several bishops from Portugal, the United States, and Canada contributed this concern:

It is time to judge again on the validity of baptism as it is conferred by sects. In practice, it seems to us, when investigations have been concluded, baptism is found either doubtful or null. But, in regard to marriage, we are supposed to judge it valid. This judgment seems contradictory to everyone, with danger to souls.[5]

The question was taken up by the commission preparing the text for the document on the liturgy. Eventually, this would be called *Sacrosanctum concilium*, or the Constitution on the Sacred Liturgy, the first major proclamation of the council. In the very first draft it called for a new rite to be created "for those who are newly converted, having already been validly baptized."[6] This request appeared in the same paragraph proposing a new rite for receiving an infant who had—in

[4] Joseph Ratzinger, *The Open Circle: The Meaning of Christian Brotherhood*, trans. W. A. Glen-Doeple (New York: Sheed and Ward, 1966) 124–25.

[5] *Acta et documenta concilio oecumenico Vatican II apparando: Antepraeparatoria Appendix* 2:2,10 (17).

[6] *Acta et documenta concilio oecumenico Vatican II apparando, Praeparatoria* 2:3,279 (54).

an emergency—earlier been baptized into a parish church. At first the circumstances seem strangely dissimilar, but in both cases the council was addressing the needs of someone who was validly baptized. The placement is significant because it implied that those with a valid Protestant baptism, for example, probably needed only something equivalent to the "missing" parts of the baptismal rite—on the level of the anointing with chrism or giving a white garment, for instance.

This first draft received a variety of comments, pro and con. But when the schema was revised and presented for the first session of the council in 1962, the sentence calling for a new rite to be created "for those who are newly converted, having already been validly baptized," was unchanged.[7]

The commission working on the text made a few revisions based on the comments of the bishops and presented it to them in 1963. The revised text changed "newly converted" to "converted" and added a reason for the ritual:

> A new rite should be created for the sake of those already validly
> baptized, having converted to the holy Catholic Church, by which
> it may be signified that they are admitted to the communion of
> the Church.[8]

The structure of the rite was still unclear, but something new had to be drawn up. The old form no longer fit the new reality. This sentence survived the final emendations to the liturgy constitution intact. On December 4, 1963, the council approved the Constitution on the Sacred Liturgy (*Sacrosanctum concilium*) by a vote of 2,147 to 4.[9]

Other documents of the council influenced the shape of this rite. Concerning members of Eastern Orthodox Churches, for example, this reception was to be kept simple:

[7] Francisco Gil Hellín, *Concilii Vaticani II synopsis in ordinem redigens schemata cum relationibus necnon Patrum orationes atque animadversiones: Constitutio de Sacra Liturgia Sacrosanctum concilium* (Vatican City: Libreria Editrice Vaticana, 2003) 212.

[8] *Acta et documenta concilio oecumenico Vatican II apparando: Acta Synodalia* 2:2,553.

[9] Annibale Bugnini, *The Reform of the Liturgy 1948–1975*, trans. Matthew J. O'Connell (Collegeville: Liturgical Press, 1990) 37.

Nothing more may be demanded than what a simple profession of Catholic faith demands of those coming from separated Eastern churches to Catholic unity under the influence of the grace of the Holy Spirit.[10]

At the same session, the council fathers also proclaimed the Constitution on the Church (*Lumen gentium*). It includes a dramatic statement recognizing the positive relationship among communities who share a common baptism:

> Concerning those who, having been baptized, are adorned with the Christian name, but who do not profess the entire faith (*integram fidem*) or do not preserve the unity of communion under the Successor of Peter, the Church recognizes that it is joined to them for many reasons. For there are many who hold the Sacred Scriptures in honor as the norm of believing and living, and who manifest a sincere religious zeal, who lovingly believe in God the almighty Father and in Christ the Savior, the Son of God, who are signed in baptism, by which they are conjoined to Christ, and who even recognize and receive other sacraments in their own Churches or ecclesial communities.[11]

This paragraph, while acknowledging the differences that exist between the Catholic Church and other communities, at the same time recognizes the grace of God at work in many of their members because of their baptism. Most significant is what the paragraph does not say. It never uses the word "heresy." The terms, as Father Ratzinger had predicted, needed to be adjusted. Pope Paul VI once referred to those outside the Catholic Church with valid baptisms as "many brothers and sisters separated from the communion of the Apostolic See."[12]

Perhaps nothing captured the spirit of the ecumenical movement in the Catholic Church better than the Decree on Ecumenism (*Unitatis redintegratio*), which the council fathers approved on the same day as these other documents in 1964. Although distinctions were still carefully drawn, one senses the heady excitement of a new day in the relationship among the various Christian bodies.

---

[10] *Orientalium ecclesiarum* 25, AAS 57 (1965) 83–84.
[11] *Lumen gentium* 15, AAS 57 (1965) 19.
[12] *Ecclesiam suam* (6 August 1964), AAS 56 (1964) 656.

Those who now are born into such communities and are instructed with the faith of Christ cannot be accused of the sin of separation, and the Catholic Church embraces them with fraternal reverence and love. For these who believe in Christ and have received baptism correctly are established in a certain, although not complete (*perfecta*), communion with the Catholic Church.[13]

Distinctions clear to the early church and lost to the Middle Ages were being restored: Someone born and baptized in another Christian community cannot be accused of sin. This same decree apologized for sins that obstructed the union of Christians, speaking with a spirit of sorrow that the Catholic Church rarely shows in ecumenical dialogue:

Concerning sins against unity the witness of St. John still has value: "If we say that we have not sinned, we make God a liar, and his word is not in us" (1 John 1:10). Therefore we ask pardon from God and from our separated brothers and sisters with a humble prayer, as we also forgive those who trespass against us.[14]

Still, even this document called the movement from a separated ecclesial community to the Catholic Church "reconciliation."

It is clear that the work of preparation and reconciliation of those individuals who desire full Catholic communion is different in nature from an ecumenical undertaking. But there is no opposition because both proceed from the marvelous direction of God.[15]

This decree therefore found no conflict between "reconciling" those seeking full communion and working for ecumenism. Rita Ferrone's comment on this passage says even more optimistically, "ecumenism aims toward a future church that will not be identical to any one of the church bodies that now exist; the aim is to gather into one all the traditions and institutions that are truly the work of Christ's Spirit."[16]

Yet the decree seems to imply that the movement from baptism to communion is a movement the Catholic Church has already accom-

---

[13] *Unitatis redintegratio* 3, AAS 57:93.

[14] Ibid., 7, AAS 57:97.

[15] Ibid., 4, AAS 57:95.

[16] Ferrone, "Reception in Context," 35 (see chap.1, n. 29).

plished. Others have yet to be completely incorporated into that plan of salvation. The Decree on Ecumenism does not precisely state Ferrone's vision, but its view is not incompatible, especially if one considers that complete eucharistic communion happens not just with individuals but when all Christians share it:

> Baptism therefore establishes a sacramental bond of unity thriving among those who have been reborn through it. Nevertheless baptism of itself is no more than an entrance and a beginning (*dumtaxat initium et exordium*), which indeed tends toward acquiring the fullness of life in Christ. Therefore baptism is ordered toward a complete profession of faith, toward complete incorporation into the plan of salvation, as Christ himself wanted it, toward the complete introduction, therefore, into eucharistic communion.[17]

The council thus affirmed the validity of baptism in separated ecclesial communities (e.g., Protestant and Anglican churches) as well as the unity that baptism established with the Catholic Church. However, the council also expressed that a division in communion remained. Striving for words to define the relationship between the Catholic and Protestant churches, the council discontinued the accusation of heresy and replaced it with the expression, "a certain, although not complete, communion."

But in search of a theology of baptism, the Decree on Ecumenism called it "no more than an entrance and a beginning." This qualification affects the theology and practice of sacraments in the Catholic Church, as well as its recognition of baptism in other churches. The Catholic Church could feel comfortable calling baptism "no more than an entrance and a beginning" because it practices infant baptism but defers confirmation and first communion. Even among Catholics, the baptism of infants is only an entrance and a beginning toward communion.

Still, the Catholic Church was affirming the baptism of other ecclesial bodies. This recognition of a common baptism had an immediate effect on the church's ceremonies. Even before the new rite of reception was composed, Pope Paul VI authorized some changes in the rite of supplying ceremonies for a person already baptized:

---

[17] Ibid., 22, AAS 57:105–6.

In the order of supplying the omitted parts for a baptized adult, which is found in the Roman Ritual title II, chapter 6, the exorcisms which are found under number 5 (*Exi abe eo*), 15 (*Ergo, maledicte diabole*), 17 (*Audi, maledicte satana*), 19 (*Exorcizo te – Ergo, maledicte diabole*), 21 (*Ergo, maledicte diabole*), 23 (*Ergo maledicte diabole*), 25 (*Exorcizo te – Ergo, maledicte diabole*), 31 (*Nec te latet*) and 35 (*Exi, immunde spiritus*), are omitted.[18]

In the history of initiation, exorcisms are a prebaptismal ritual. They were not appropriate to this rite because the baptism already received was valid.

A new respect for other religions was growing. Even Vatican II's 1965 Declaration on Religious Liberty noted that as a sign of the times, "People of diverse culture and religion are being drawn together in stronger relationships."[19]

POSTCONCILIAR ACTIVITY

The First Ecumenical Directory was promulgated in 1967, clarifying the Catholic Church's relationships with other ecclesial bodies of the East and West. For example, it affirmed the validity of the baptism of separated Eastern Christians and urged the simplest procedures on behalf of those who sought Catholic unity.

The validity of baptism conferred among separated Eastern Christians cannot be called into doubt. It is enough therefore to establish that it happened.[20]

The same document also criticized the former practice of baptizing conditionally those whose baptism should be considered valid.

The practice of indiscriminately baptizing conditionally all who desire full communion with the Catholic Church cannot be approved. For the sacrament of baptism cannot be repeated, and therefore baptism is not permitted to be conferred again conditionally unless there is a prudent doubt about the fact or the validity of the baptism formerly conferred.[21]

---

[18] Sacred Congregations of Rites, *Inter Oecumenici* 3:2/63, AAS 56 (1964) 892.
[19] *Dignitatis humanae* 15, AAS 58 (1966) 941.
[20] *Ad totam ecclesiam* 12, AAS 59 (1967) 579.
[21] Ibid., 14, AAS 59:580.

Where conditional baptism must be administered, "it should be conferred in a private form."[22]

Furthermore, the directory separated into a distinct category those Catholics who publicly abjured faith. These need absolution, but not those born into other Christian churches:

> According to the thinking of the Decree on Ecumenism, brothers and sisters born and baptized outside the visible communion of the Catholic Church should be carefully distinguished from those who, though baptized in the Catholic Church, knowingly and publicly abjure its faith. For according to the Decree, "Those who now are born into such communities and are instructed with the faith of Christ cannot be accused of the sin of separation" (3). For this reason, absent such blame, if they wish to accept the Catholic faith on their own free will, they do not need to be absolved from the punishment of excommunication, but, after a profession of faith has been made, according to the norms established by the local Ordinary, they may be admitted to the full communion of the Catholic Church.[23]

Here, those formerly considered "heretics" are called "brothers and sisters." They are not sinners. They do not require reconciliation. Nor do they need to abjure from heresy.[24] But they needed some ritual, and the development of that text fell to the Consilium.

[22] Ibid., 15.
[23] Ibid., 19, AAS 59:581.
[24] Ibid., 20.

Chapter 4

The Development of the New Rite

The Consilium for Carrying Out the Constitution on the Sacred Liturgy assigned the development of the new rite of reception to study groups XXII and XXIII, headed by Balthasar Fischer and Pierre-Marie Gy respectively. These two wanted to work in league with the ecumenical movement. They sent a preliminary letter to their consultors in 1964 listing among the diverse questions connected with the celebration of baptism, "a new order of reception into the church of those validly baptized, having converted to the Catholic sacraments" (c.4). Furthermore, they noted: "It seems that the order of receiving those newly converted to the Catholic sacraments should be prepared after advice has been gathered with the Secretariat for the Union of Christians (4)."[1] Another letter posed some special questions for discussion, including this one: "How should one envisage the conditional baptism (if necessary) of catechumens coming from Churches separated from Rome?"[2]

Consultors met in Trier in 1967 and discussed several issues relating to the reception of validly baptized Christians. One of the first proposals would have included the rite of reception in the Easter Vigil:

> It seems to be appropriate to insert the celebration of reception into the paschal mystery, so that it might have its climax at the Paschal

---

[1] Balthasar Fischer and Pierre-Marie Gy, Letter *Omnibus Consultoribus*, 21 July 1964, pp. 12 and 14. Archives of the International Commission on English in the Liturgy, Washington DC.

[2] Fischer and Gy, Letter to the consultors, 23 August 1964, D16, p. 6. Archives of the International Commission on English in the Liturgy, Washington DC.

Vigil. For Christ died, rose and instituted the most holy Eucharist so that he might gather all people into the full unity of baptism.[3]

From the Decree on Ecumenism, the consultors understood that all baptized Christians were considered to be in a certain incomplete union with the Catholic Church. That union would be made complete in two sacraments: confirmation and Eucharist:

> Moreover, since it concerns people already baptized who must be brought into full communion with the Church [sic, *plenam commu-nionem cum Ecclesia*], it is fitting that the rite of reception takes both its euchological and theological foundation from their baptism, for which thanks must be given to God. Then it is necessary to signify the relationship of baptism (and therefore of the new rite) with the sacraments of Christian fullness, namely *confirmation* and the *most holy Eucharist*.[4]

In admitting Eastern Orthodox Christians to Catholic communion, their initiation was already considered complete.[5] They would not be confirmed.

The study group discussed handlaying at length. If the celebrant imposed hands on the candidate during the rite of reception, the gesture might be confused with reconciliation and confirmation. The group wanted to include confirmation in the public celebration of the rite, but the question of handlaying was left unresolved at the meeting in Trier.[6]

In the group's draft of the liturgy, the one to be admitted (*admittendus*) approached the celebrant. The celebrant gave thanks for this person's baptism, the foundation of admission. Then the person professed his or her faith. The celebrant placed both hands on the head of the one being received and recited a formula,

---

[3] Coetus a Studiis XXII, Schema 236, De Rituali 22 (11 July 1967) *Consilium ad exsequendam constitutionem de Sacra Liturgia*, 2b, p. 6. Archives of the International Commission on English in the Liturgy, Washington DC. Hereafter, Schema 236.

[4] Ibid.

[5] McManus, Letter to Hotchkin with attached proposal, 1 August 1967, Archives of the Bishops' Committee on the Liturgy, National Conference of Catholic Bishops (U.S.A.), Washington DC. Cited in Sieverding, *Ordo admissionis* 225 (see ch. 2, n. 2).

[6] Schema 236.

which at the same time expresses reception into the Church and the forgiveness of sins (which the *admittendus* earlier has confessed privately to the celebrant.) It is done this way, however, so that it may clearly appear that the reception is not to be identified with the forgiveness of sins; personal sins are forgiven the one received.[7]

The liturgy would continue with confirmation (except for those who had already validly received it), prayers, and the Eucharist.

Not everyone agreed with these proposals. Notably, Frederick McManus, an esteemed American liturgist, canonist, and theologian, argued against features that made reception resemble baptism. Baptism is the "basis of the unity already existing and . . . the present celebration is rather an admission to communion of a person hitherto separated or not in full communion."[8] He also challenged the idea of celebrating reception at the Easter Vigil. "In the past this reception into communion has been treated as a 'conversion' with its own kind of catechumenate." Any elements of the rite "that would cast doubt upon the baptism of other Christians which has been properly celebrated, or upon the religious life they have been leading prior to their reception into communion" must be avoided.[9] He also recommended that the profession of faith be made together with the entire community, using a common formula such as the Nicene Creed or the Apostles Creed.[10] Regarding handlaying, McManus feared it would be misunderstood.

> It seems to me to be entirely impossible not to identify the act of admission with the forgiveness of sins if the imposition of hands is the single sign of these two. It is, moreover, not clear to me why there must be a public remission of sins in these circumstances; if there ever is an occasion for private confession and absolution, it is this—when the intent of the new rite is to avoid judging whether the person has been guilty in the act of separation from the Church.[11]

[7] McManus to Hotchkin.

[8] F. McManus, Letter to B. Fischer, 18 August 1967, Archives of the Bishops' Committee on the Liturgy, National Conference of Catholic Bishops (U.S.A.), Washington DC. (Cited in Sieverding, *Ordo admissionis* 227).

[9] Ibid.

[10] Ibid.

[11] Ibid.

McManus proposed using a different sign for reception, such as the kiss of peace. He suggested adding "a prayer for unity and prayer for the forgiveness of sins against unity, whether they are committed by the Roman Catholic community or by others."[12]

In 1967 the study group prepared another draft for this liturgy. The wording changed from the description in *Sacrosanctum concilium* ("for the sake of those already validly baptized, having converted to the holy Catholic Church, by which it is signified that they are admitted to the communion of the Church") to this: "an order for a rite of receiving those already validly baptized into the full communion of the Catholic Church."[13] Those being received were no longer called "converts." They were not being admitted to communion, but to the full communion of the Catholic Church. These nuances reflected a newfound ecumenical sensitivity, yet a reassertion of the stance that full communion is found in the Catholic Church.

The draft asked that all appearances of triumphalism be avoided. This expression, which appears in the final version of the rite,[14] was probably suggested by the Secretariat for Christian Unity.[15] Yet the same document still permitted receiving Christians as part of the Paschal Vigil, in order to link reception to the paschal mystery.[16] The entire community would recite the profession of faith together with the one being received, who would usually be confirmed in the same ceremony.[17]

Regarding handlaying, the draft suggested that it be included only if confirmation did not follow (e.g., in the case of Eastern Orthodox Christians). But it recognized that the gesture traditionally signified reconciliation:

> To signify reception according to the most ancient custom, which the Roman Pontifical still foresees in Part III for reconciliation, the

---

[12] Ibid.

[13] Coetus a Studiis XXII, Schema 252, De Rituali 24 (3 November 1967), *Consilium ad exsequendam constitutionem de Sacra Liturgia*, p. 1. Archives of the International Commission on English in the Liturgy, Washington DC. Hereafter, Schema 252. The change was made to match the wording of the 14 May 1967 ecumenical directory.

[14] RCIA 475/2.

[15] Sieverding, *Ordo admissionis*, 234.

[16] Schema 252, 4, p. 3. The original document said that their first communion "most fittingly takes place" at the Paschal Vigil.

[17] Ibid.

imposition of a hand is used. The celebrant places his right hand upon the head of the one being received, saying at the same time, "I admit you into the full communion of the Catholic Church." Then he takes the hands of the one received between his own hands (or if circumstances permit he embraces him [her]). Another gesture that similarly expresses a friendly welcome may be substituted in place of this one, according to regions and circumstances, with permission of the Ordinary.[18]

If the celebrant was to confirm the candidate, he should impose hands only once:

But if the one received has not yet been confirmed, and the one receiving is a bishop or presbyter enjoying the faculty of confirming (cf. n.6), he confirms the candidate at once with an appropriately brief rite. He does it this way so that one and the same imposition of the hand receives and confirms him (her), placing in front of the formula of confirmation the words, "I admit you into the full communion of the Catholic Church." In this case, the greeting, (see 13 below), happens after confirmation.[19]

Two weeks later, the study group strengthened the opinion that the liturgy of reception should take place within Mass. The words for the appropriateness of the Easter Vigil for this celebration changed from "most fittingly takes place" to "fittingly may take place."[20] McManus stated that confirmation was essential before communion:

If the adult who is baptized (or the adult who is received into full communion with the Church) is not confirmed on the occasion of his baptism (or reception), he should not be admitted to the Eucharist.[21]

---

[18] Schema 252, 13, p. 5.

[19] Schema 252, 14, p. 5. A footnote in the original cites "Hippolytus 1.c. (Botte 54)"—*The Apostolic Tradition*—as its source: "And consigning the forehead he offers a kiss."

[20] Coetus a Studiis XXII, Schema 256, De Rituali 25 (20 November 1967), *Consilium ad exsequendam constitutionem de Sacra Liturgia* 4, p. 3. Archives of the International Commission on English in the Liturgy, Washington DC.

[21] Notes of McManus found in the archives of the International Commission on English in the Liturgy, Washington, DC. (Cited in Sieverding, *Ordo admissionis*, 241.)

The opinion that confirmation must precede Eucharist would seem obvious to the Eastern Churches. Yet it has little foundation in the liturgical practice of the West. Nonetheless, the opinion was sustained in the United States in the National Statutes.[22]

In 1968 another draft was proposed, making a few changes, some of which would be changed again. For example, the formula spoken by the priest for the act of reception was originally composed as a prayer addressed to God:

> Receive, Lord,
> this your servant,
> whom you have led here in your mercy,
> so that he (she) may have full communion with us
> in the truth he (she) has professed
> in the presence of your family.[23]

According to a footnote, this formula was inspired by one in the Syrian Jacobite tradition, from the Order to be Observed Toward Him (Her) Who Converts from the Heresies of the Nestorians, Chalcedonians, or Julianists, or from Any of the Other Heresies which Thrive Among Christians. That text ran as follows:

> Now, Lord, Lover of People, make us acceptable in our ministry, and raise up this your servant who converts to you and affirms your truth after formerly affirming the error of the heresies that he (she) held, and who has confessed your truth in the presence of our weakness. Grant him (her), Lord, forgiveness of sins.[24]

Thus, the study group lifted a text from the tradition of converting heretics and adjusted it to fit modern circumstances. The new prayer concerned a "servant" who was seeking "full communion," not a "convert" turning from "heresy," who needed "forgiveness."

---

[22] National Statutes 35 (see Appendix III of RCIA). "The confirmation of such candidates for reception should not be deferred, nor should they be admitted to the eucharist until they are confirmed."

[23] Coetus a Studiis XXII, Schema 276, De Rituali, 26 (8 March 1968), *Consilium ad exsequendam constitutionem de Sacra Liturgia* 14, p. 7. Archives of the International Commission on English in the Liturgy, Washington DC. Hereafter, Schema 276.

[24] *Ritus Orientalium: Coptorum, Syrorum et Armenorum, in administrandis sacramentis*, ed. Henricus Denziger, (Wurzburg 1863) 1:466.

The draft of the liturgy also suggested that the entire community greet the newly received person in a friendly way. A footnote gave this reason for doing so:

> [This comes f]rom a very ancient custom; for example, the newly baptized or a guest is not greeted by the faithful until after they will have prayed with him (her) for the first time.[25]

The origin of this "very ancient custom" is not clear. It probably blends a passage from the second-century martyr Justin with one from the Rule of Benedict. Justin says of the first part of the eucharistic gathering, "When the prayers are concluded we exchange the kiss."[26] Benedict says,

> Once a guest has been announced, this person is to be met by the superior or the brothers with all the obligation of charity. First they are to pray together and thus be united with one another in peace. The kiss of peace is not to be offered first without the preliminary prayer because of demonic deceptions.[27]

However, these sources do not support the ritual at hand. If the greeting during the rite of reception today is meant to parallel the case in Justin, it would disaffirm the baptism of the candidates; being validly baptized, they were eligible for the sign of peace *before* they were received. This gesture is better explained as a sign of welcome, which seems to be what Benedict has in mind. However, Benedict is describing the arrival of a guest in the monastery, and not the reception of a baptized Christian into full communion. And he recommends praying before kissing so that the kiss will not be misinterpreted as a temptation to sin. In today's rite, the greeting functions as a human sign of welcome, and it does not seem to need historical liturgical precedent.

When the study group next met, its members prepared the final draft for the rite of reception. A few more changes were implemented. The introduction now quoted the Decree on Ecumenism, in turn quoting Acts of the Apostles 15:28, that "for restoring communion and

---

[25] Schema 276, 18, footnote 12, p. 8.

[26] Justin, *Apologia* 1:65; cf. *Catechism of the Catholic Church*, 2nd ed. (Vatican City: 2000) 1345.

[27] Paul Turner's translation of the Latin text of RB 53.3–9 in *The Rule of St. Benedict*, ed. Timothy Fry (Collegeville: Liturgical Press, 1981) 256.

unity 'no greater burden than necessary'" should be imposed.[28] As a consequence, the reception of Eastern Orthodox Christians was to happen with a simple profession of Catholic faith.[29]

For the first time, this draft mentions the Mass for the Unity of the Church.[30] Its presidential prayers and Scripture readings could be used at times to accompany the rite of reception. This further demonstrates the council's opinion that the goals of ecumenism and reception are not opposed. Even as one Christian is being received into the full communion of the Catholic Church, so the church prays for the unity of all Christians.

The study group made suggestions for the homily. Recalling that reception occurs within the context of the paschal mystery, the suggested homily mentions all three sacraments of initiation:

> The reception takes place after the homily in which mention is gratefully made of baptism as the foundation of reception, of the confirmation about to be received or having been received, and also of the most holy Eucharist to be celebrated for the first time with Catholics.[31]

Even so, the text no longer recommended the Easter Vigil as the appropriate time of celebration. That suggestion was removed from consideration.

The formula for reception was also changed to highlight the activity of the Holy Spirit. The subtle change from professing "truth" to professing "faith" erased another inference that the one being admitted formerly adhered to a heresy. No longer a prayer text, it became a declaration:

> The Lord who brought you here in his mercy
> receives you, N.,
> so that you may have full communion with us in the Holy Spirit
> in the faith you have professed in the presence of this his family.[32]

---

[28] Coetus a Studiis XXII, Schema 290, De Rituali 28 (21 April 1968), *Consilium ad exsequendam constitutionem de Sacra Liturgia* 1, p. 3. Archives of the International Commission on English in the Liturgy, Washington DC. Hereafter, Schema 290.

[29] Schema 290, 2, p. 3.

[30] Ibid.

[31] Schema 290, 12b, p. 6.

[32] Schema 290, 14, p. 7.

The draft also permitted a sensitive change if the reception took place outside of Mass: "If the one who was received had the custom in his (her) communion of adding to the Lord's Prayer the phrase, 'for thine is the kingdom . . . ,' it may be added here."[33] It would already be included in the liturgy if the reception were taking place at Mass.

In one last meeting in 1968 the study group made a few final adjustments. For example, when the celebrant invites forward the one to be received, the previous draft had him say, "I invite you now with great joy. . . ."[34] But this was now thought too "triumphalistic," so the revised text took an entirely different approach: "N., after careful thought you have requested of your own free will to be received. . . ."[35] The change stresses the free decision of the candidate, not the feeling of the church.

The candidate's formula following the profession of faith also changed. The one being received, having professed faith with the community, was to say alone: "I believe and profess all that the holy Catholic Church believes and teaches to be revealed by God." The study group thought this was too abstract and added one more word: "I believe and profess all that the holy Catholic Church believes, teaches and proclaims to be revealed by God."[36] It can be debated whether or not adding the word "proclaims" removes abstraction, but the change remained.

The finished product, the *editio typica* for this ritual, was published as an appendix to the *Ordo Initiationis Christianæ Adultorum* in 1972 under the title *Ordo admissionis valide iam baptizorum in plenam communionem ecclesiæ catholicæ*. A few more changes are noticeable. The prohibition against repeating baptism was included, as well as the discipline concerning conditional baptism. The formula of reception was expanded with the phrase "into the Catholic Church," to clarify the point of this reception:

[33] Schema 290, p. 9a.

[34] Schema 290, 12, p. 6.

[35] Coetus a Studiis XXII, Adnexa ad: Schema 290, De Rituali 28 (29 April 1968), *Consilium ad exsequendam constitutionem de Sacra Liturgia* 7, p. 2. Archives of the International Commission on English in the Liturgy, Washington DC. Hereafter, Schema 290a.

[36] Schema 290a, 8, p. 2.

The Lord, who brought you here in his mercy, receives you, N.,
into the Catholic Church, so that you may have full communion
with us in the Holy Spirit in the faith you have professed in the
presence of this his family.[37]

Through many conversations, ideas, changes, and deletions, the rite
envisioned by the Second Vatican Council had finally been published
as an appendix to the *Ordo initiationis christianæ adultorum*. This placement is noteworthy. *Sacrosanctum concilium* first conceived the rite
together with a ceremony for infants baptized in emergency. It ended
up as an appendix to the rites for unbaptized adults. Yet it is a *tertium
quid*. It was probably included with the catechumenate rites because
they were being re-created at the same time by virtually the same
study group members. There was considerable concern that those who
were already baptized should not be confused with those who were
not. The *editio typica* of the rite of reception probably could have stood
on its own, instead of as an appendix to another rite. In some ways, it
is a quirk of history that the restoration of the catechumenate occurred
at the same time as the creation of the rite of reception. One wonders if
these rites had been developed even a few decades apart from each
other, whether those validly baptized would have been thought of as a
group so strongly related to catechumens.

---

[37] *Ordo admissionis* 16. Author's translation.

Chapter 5

The English Translation in the United States

PROVISIONAL TEXTS

A provisional English translation for the United States appeared in 1976. It came, not as an appendix to the provisional translation of the Rite of Christian Initiation of Adults, but as a separate publication bearing the title Rite of Reception of Baptized Christians into Full Communion with the Catholic Church.[1]

A year later, the American bishops published "The Reception of Baptized Christians and the Rite of Baptism During the Easter Vigil."[2] The preface explained its purpose:

> The Easter Vigil is the proper occasion for the celebration of the sacraments of initiation. In some places not only adults are baptized and confirmed on this occasion but infants as well. Even the reception of adults into the church has been included in the Holy Saturday celebration of some parishes.
>
> Whereas the *Sacramentary* does indicate the place for the liturgy of baptism and confirmation in the Easter Vigil service (Part Three: Liturgy of Baptism) it does not provide the necessary liturgical rites. This insert has been prepared in order to provide those who preside at the Vigil of Easter with the texts that are required for the celebration of baptism, confirmation or reception of adults.
>
> This material should not be interpreted as a replacement of the pre-baptismal catechumenate (See *Rite of Christian Initiation of*

[1] Washington: United States Conference of Catholic Bishops, 1976.

[2] "The Reception of Baptized Christians and the Rite of Baptism During the Easter Vigil." Washington: National Conference of Catholic Bishops, Bishops' Committee on the Liturgy, 1977.

Adults) with its proper stages of initiation. Neither does this material propose that the reception of candidates during the Easter Vigil become normative. On the contrary, a more appropriate time might be selected to maintain the clear distinction between the unbaptized catechumens and the baptized Christians requesting full reception into the Roman Catholic Church.

The Easter Vigil is already a service rich in symbolism and meaning. The inclusion of additional rites must keep this in mind and unnecessary repetitions must be avoided when possible.

. . . Only the newly baptized infants receive the post-baptismal anointing. It is presumed that if adults are baptized or received into the Church at the Vigil they will also be confirmed during it.[3]

In this insert, after the homily, the baptismal candidates and godparents are called forward for the litany and blessing water. "After the blessing of the water the candidates for reception are called forth with their sponsors to join the baptismal candidates."[4] This would be changed in the 1988 edition of the *Rite of Christian Initiation of Adults*, which does not bring the baptized candidates forward until the baptisms have taken place.

Once the candidates for baptism and reception are standing together, "The celebrant, in his own words, invites all the candidates to reject sin and make a profession of faith."[5] All these candidates make the baptismal promises together. Then, "The celebrant addresses all of those to be received into full communion: 'Do you believe and profess all that the holy Catholic Church believes, teaches, and proclaims to be revealed by God?'" The candidates respond, "I do," and the celebrant receives each of them, repeating the text for the act of reception ("N., the Lord receives you into the Catholic Church. . . .").[6] The rite of baptism then follows. Afterward, all those eligible for it receive the sacrament of confirmation and, "The Easter Vigil continues with the renewal of baptismal promises."[7]

The title of the 1976 provisional text changed when the official English translation was approved in 1988. Formerly called the Rite of Reception of Baptized Christians into Full Communion with the

[3] Ibid., [2].
[4] Ibid., [3].
[5] Ibid.
[6] Ibid., [4].
[7] Ibid., [5–6].

Catholic Church, it was now the Rite of Reception into the Full Communion of the Catholic Church. The earlier title could be misconstrued to mean that it was possible for someone remaining outside the Catholic Church to have communion with it. The corrected title implies that there is one communion. It is full. And it is shared in the Catholic Church. One obtains regular access to eucharistic communion in the church after one has been received into the full communion of the church.[8]

Of interest, the new English translation of the title still omitted the Latin word *valide*, probably because it seemed tautologous. Either one is baptized or not; an "invalid baptism" is not a baptism.

THE NATIONAL STATUTES

As early as 1986 the National Conference of Catholic Bishops had approved National Statutes for the Catechumenate. Almost at the very beginning, the bishops said that distinctions in terminology should be made between the baptized and the unbaptized:

> The term "catechumen" should be strictly reserved for the unbaptized who have been admitted into the order of catechumens, the term "convert" should be reserved strictly for those converted from unbelief to Christian belief and never used of those baptized Christians who are received into the full communion of the Catholic Church.[9]

The bishops did not offer an alternative word for those formerly called "converts." In popular usage, these precisions have never completely caught on. It is still common to hear even Christians received into the Catholic Church call themselves "converts." They are not casting a negative judgment on the validity of the baptism they received; they are just using a traditional word. Still, the bishops make a critical theological point.

Regarding the preparation of baptized candidates, the bishops said it "should be determined according to the individual case,"[10] so the length of time should vary from one candidate to another. The bishops expected the candidates to celebrate the sacrament of reconciliation

---

[8] *Rite of Christian Initiation of Adults*, various editions, 1988.
[9] National Statutes (see Appendix III of RCIA) 2.
[10] Ibid., 30.

before their reception, but not because candidates need absolution from heresy. By recommending frequent confession in the same statute, the bishops situated reconciliation in the context of what it is—the forgiveness of personal sins:

> The celebration of the sacrament of reconciliation with candidates for reception into full communion is to be carried out at a time prior to and distinct from the celebration of the rite of reception. As part of the formation of such candidates, they should be encouraged in the frequent celebration of this sacrament.[11]

The bishops recommended that the rite of reception not take place at the Easter Vigil, but these strong words, somewhat buried in the National Statutes, were easily overlooked:

> It is preferable that the reception into full communion not take place at the Easter Vigil lest there be any confusion of such baptized Christians with the candidates for baptism, possible misunderstanding of or even reflection upon the sacrament of baptism celebrated in another Church or ecclesial community, or any perceived triumphalism in the liturgical welcome into the Catholic eucharistic community.[12]

The bishops softened this position in the very next statute:

> Nevertheless if there are both catechumens to be baptized and baptized Christians to be received into full communion at the Vigil, for pastoral reasons and in view of the Vigil's being the principal annual celebration of the church, the combined rite is to be followed. . . . A clear distinction should be maintained during the celebration between candidates for sacramental initiation and candidates for reception into full communion, and ecumenical sensitivities should be carefully respected.[13]

THE OPTIONAL RITES
The 1988 English translation for use in the United States included a number of approved adaptations. These have been used many times

---

[11] Ibid., 36.
[12] Ibid., 33.
[13] Ibid., 34.

for pastoral advantage. But compromises produced inconsistencies in their composition, and their celebration has carried some drawbacks.

Modeled on the catechumenate rites, they were called "Optional Rites for Baptized but Uncatechized Adults." But they may be and have often been used even for those baptized Christians who were already catechized—sometimes without giving them an option. These rites seeded the perception that baptized candidates should be received at the Easter Vigil, when catechumens were to be baptized.

The Rite of Welcoming

The first of these, the Rite of Welcoming the Candidates, is based on the Rite of Acceptance into the Order of Catechumens. It shares the nature of a first liturgy that introduces candidates to the larger community, which hears about their intentions. The introduction recommends setting specified days throughout the year for the celebration of this ceremony.[14]

OUTLINE OF THE RITES	
RITE OF ACCEPTANCE INTO THE ORDER OF CATECHUMENS	RITE OF WELCOMING THE CANDIDATES
RECEIVING THE CANDIDATES	WELCOMING THE CANDIDATES
Greeting	Greeting
Opening Dialogue	Opening Dialogue
Candidates' First Acceptance of the Gospel	Candidates' Declaration of Intent
Affirmation by the Sponsors and the Assembly[15]	Affirmation by the Sponsors and the Assembly
Signing of the Candidates with the Cross	Signing of the Candidates with the Cross
Invitation to the Celebration of the Word of God	

[14] RCIA 414.

[15] When the unbaptized candidates are children of catechetical age, their parents or sponsors speak on their behalf (RCIA 265).

RITE OF ACCEPTANCE INTO THE ORDER OF CATECHUMENS	RITE OF WELCOMING THE CANDIDATES
LITURGY OF THE WORD	LITURGY OF THE WORD
Instruction	Instruction
Readings	Readings
Homily	Homily
[Presentation of a Bible]	[Presentation of a Bible]
Intercessions for the Catechumens	General Intercessions
Prayer over the Catechumens	Prayer over the Candidates
Dismissal of the Catechumens	

Whereas the Rite of Acceptance into the Order of Catechumens begins outdoors to symbolize the entrance of the unbaptized into the church,[16] the Rite of Welcoming the Candidates begins indoors: "Because they are already numbered among the baptized, the candidates are seated in a prominent place among the faithful."[17]

The celebrant greets the candidates and explains the significance of the ceremony.[18] He asks, "What is your name?" and then, "What do you ask of God's Church?" Candidates answer in their own words, but the suggested response is laconic: "To be accepted as a candidate for catechetical instruction leading to confirmation and Eucharist (or: reception into the full communion of the Catholic Church)."[19] The candidates declare their intention to reflect more deeply on the mystery of their baptism, to listen with the community to the Scriptures, and to join in a life of prayer and service.[20] The sponsors and the assembly indicate their support, and the celebrant prays in thanksgiving to God for these servants, "already consecrated" in baptism.[21] The celebrant traces the sign of the cross on the forehead of the candidates "as a reminder" of their baptism; catechists and sponsors may do the same.

[16] RCIA 48.
[17] RCIA 416.
[18] RCIA 417.
[19] RCIA 418.
[20] RCIA 419.
[21] RCIA 420.

While the community sings an acclamation, other senses may be signed.[22] These first ceremonies conclude with a pertinent prayer or the opening prayer of the Mass of the day.

In the Rite of Acceptance into the Order of *Catechumens*, a cross may be offered to the new catechumens at this point of the parallel rite.[23] That gesture was omitted in the rite of Welcoming. Also in the Rite of Acceptance the catechumens are invited from outside into the church before the Liturgy of the Word,[24] but this invitation is omitted from the Rite of Welcoming because the candidates are already inside the building.

"The celebrant next speaks briefly to the candidates and their sponsors, helping them to understand the dignity of God's word proclaimed and heard in the church."[25] This statement presumes that the candidates are uncatechized, and that they have little or no experience with the word of God:

> After the readings and a homily,
>
> A book containing the gospels may be given to the candidates by the celebrant. The celebrant may use words suited to the gift presented, for example, "receive the Gospel of Jesus Christ, the Son of God." The candidates may respond in an appropriate way.[26]

This is optional and would not be appropriate for candidates familiar with the Bible.

The liturgy continues with general intercessions, some of which pray specifically for the candidates beginning their formation. They are called "general intercessions" because this is the expression for the petitions within the context of Mass; "intercessions" are made for the catechumens in the parallel rite either because the ceremony does not include Mass or because, if it does, they may be dismissed before another set of petitions, the general intercessions, are made.

The Liturgy of the Eucharist may follow. There is no indication for the dismissal of the candidates, as there would be for the unbaptized

---

[22] RCIA 422–23.
[23] RCIA 59.
[24] RCIA 60.
[25] RCIA 425.
[26] RCIA 428.

catechumens. They may remain for the Eucharist, but they may not yet partake of communion.[27]

This liturgy attempts to distinguish the status of these candidates from catechumens. But some of these details are so subtle that they will be overlooked by many churchgoers.

The Rite of Christian Initiation of Adults also permits catechumens and candidates being prepared together to celebrate a combined rite of Acceptance and Welcoming. In this case, both groups begin the liturgy outside the church, obliterating the first distinction the rite of Welcoming made.[28] The rite may begin inside, but both groups remain together. In the acceptance of the gospel and declaration of intent, the questions indicate the distinctions between the groups. The two groups are signed separately with the cross.[29] The optional presentation of a cross to the catechumens is omitted,[30] erasing another opportunity to distinguish the candidates.

Both groups are invited into the church for the Liturgy of the Word,[31] ignoring another distinction. Before the readings, the celebrant gives both groups a brief instruction about the significance of the Word of God.[32] After the readings and homily, a book containing the gospels may be presented to both groups. Both groups are included in the intercessions and their concluding prayer.

Then the catechumens—not the candidates—may be dismissed from the liturgy.[33] But the catechumens are allowed to stay; and in the context of this ceremony, more separations fail to be made if both groups remain. In practice, many parishes dismiss both groups, resulting in the same problem.

The Rite of Sending

The second optional ceremony is the Rite of Sending the Candidates for Recognition by the Bishop and for the Call to Continuing Conversion. This presumes that the diocesan Rite of Election for catechumens will be amplified to include a parallel ritual for the candidates—cus-

---

[27] RCIA 430–33.
[28] RCIA 507.
[29] RCIA 514–19.
[30] RCIA 59.
[31] RCIA 521.
[32] RCIA 522.
[33] RCIA 528AB.

tomary now in many dioceses. It also presumes that the rite of reception will be taking place at the Easter Vigil; otherwise, there would be no point in gathering the candidates on the First Sunday of Lent. The American edition of the RCIA includes an optional parish Rite of Sending for *catechumens* who will celebrate the Rite of Election.[34] This is based on material from the Rite of Election—a precelebration of Election, so that parishes can participate at home in what has become a diocesan event. The Rite of Sending the *Candidates*, then, is an adaptation of the Rite of Sending the Elect, which is itself an adaptation, in preparation for an adapted combined liturgy at the cathedral.

OUTLINE OF THE RITES	
[RITE OF] SENDING OF THE CATECHUMENS FOR ELECTION	RITE OF SENDING THE CANDIDATES FOR RECOGNITION BY THE BISHOP AND FOR THE CALL TO CONTINUING CONVERSION
Presentation of the Catechumens	Presentation of the Candidates
Affirmation by the Godparents [and the Assembly]	Affirmation by the Sponsors [and the Assembly]
Intercessions for the Catechumens	General Intercessions
Prayer over the Catechumens	Prayer over the Candidates

The parish celebration of the Rite of Sending the Candidates begins when someone presents them to the celebrant.[35] The sponsors and the assembly testify that the candidates are ready for the sacraments of confirmation and Eucharist.[36] The celebrant then addresses the candidates:

> And now, my dear friends, I address you. Your own sponsors [and this entire community] have spoken in your favor. The Church,

---

[34] RCIA 106–17.
[35] RCIA 439.
[36] RCIA 440.

in the name of Christ, accepts their testimony and sends you to Bishop N., who will exhort you to live in deeper conformity to the life of Christ.[37]

After the general intercessions and a prayer, the Liturgy of the Eucharist continues.

There is also a combined rite for sending catechumens for election and candidates for recognition by the bishop. It begins with the presentation of the catechumens and the affirmation by their godparents. The celebrant recommends them to the bishop. Catechumens may even sign the book of the elect in advance, if that is the diocesan custom.[38] Baptized candidates are not supposed to sign the book because it is a prebaptismal ritual, but in practice some dioceses permit and encourage this practice. After this come the presentation of the candidates and the affirmation by their sponsors, and the celebrant concludes with words sending them to the bishop.[39] Intercessions and prayer are made for both groups.[40] Catechumens may be dismissed before the Liturgy of the Eucharist, but in practice many parishes dismiss both catechumens and candidates.[41] In short, the combined rite of sending offers almost no distinctions between the two groups.

The Rite of Calling to Continuing Conversion

The third optional ceremony is the Rite of Calling the Candidates to Continuing Conversion. This may take place at the parish church if no catechumens are in formation. It is unlikely that an entire diocese in the United States would have no catechumens in formation, so there is no cathedral version of this ceremony without the Rite of Election. A few dioceses, however, have two cathedral ceremonies: one for catechumens and the other for candidates. The Calling of Candidates to Continuing Conversion is recommended for the beginning of Lent, promoting the idea that the rite of reception will take place at the Easter Vigil.[42]

---

[37] RCIA 441.
[38] RCIA 537–39.
[39] RCIA 540–42.
[40] RCIA 543–44.
[41] RCIA 545AB.
[42] RCIA 447–48.

OUTLINE OF THE RITES	
RITE OF ELECTION OR ENROLLMENT OF NAMES	RITE OF CALLING THE CANDIDATES TO CONTINUING CONVERSION
Presentation of the Catechumens	Presentation of the Candidates for Confirmation and Eucharist
Affirmation by the Godparents [and the Assembly]	Affirmation by the Sponsors [and the Assembly]
Invitation and Enrollment of Names	
Act of Admission or Election	Act of Recognition
Intercessions for the Elect	General Intercessions
Prayer over the Elect	Prayer over the Candidates
Dismissal of the Elect	

After the homily, someone presents the candidates to the celebrant.[43] The sponsors make their affirmation,[44] and the celebrant makes this statement:

> N. and N., the Church recognizes your desire (to be sealed with the gift of the Holy Spirit and) to have a place at Christ's eucharistic table. Join with us this Lent in a spirit of repentance. Hear the Lord's call to conversion and be faithful to your baptismal covenant.[45]

He asks the sponsors to take the candidates into their care. The general intercessions of the Mass follow, and prayer is made over the candidates. The Liturgy of the Eucharist may continue.[46]

A combined rite is also included. Although it is designed to take place at Mass, in practice it usually occurs as a Word service. After the homily, the two rites follow in sequence: first, the rite of election,[47]

[43] RCIA 451.
[44] RCIA 452.
[45] RCIA 454.
[46] RCIA 454–58.
[47] RCIA 551–54.

then the call to continuing conversion.[48] Both the elect and the candidates are included in the intercessions and prayer at the end.[49] If there is to be a Liturgy of the Eucharist, the elect are dismissed.[50] Thus, in the combined rite the two groups are handled separately, but within the same ceremony, at the same time and place, with the same readings and songs.

The introduction says the presiding celebrant is usually the bishop or his delegate,[51] whereas it had permitted a priest to preside when the call to conversion is celebrated separately. This obscures another potential distinction in the preparation of catechumens and candidates. The combined rite does not explicitly say that the ceremony takes place at the cathedral, but this is deduced from the rubric that the bishop presides. When the rite of election is celebrated without the call to continuing conversion, the introduction says clearly, "The rite should take place in the cathedral church, in a parish church or, if necessary, in some other suitable and fitting place."[52] But the word "cathedral" was added to this sentence in the American edition of the RCIA. Still, the rite calls for the bishop to preside, and it is logical to conclude that it would normally take place at the cathedral. The rite takes place elsewhere in dioceses where the cathedral has less seating than another place, or where the diocesan territory is so far flung that the rite is repeated regionally.

By situating the combined rite on the First Sunday of Lent,[53] the American edition presumes that parishes will celebrate the rite of reception at the Easter Vigil, in combination with baptisms.

The Penitential Rite

The fourth optional rite for baptized candidates is the Penitential Rite (Scrutiny). Because scrutinies were designed specifically for the unbaptized, a different ceremony was devised for baptized candidates:

---

[48] RCIA 555–57.
[49] RCIA 558–59.
[50] RCIA 560AB.
[51] RCIA 548.
[52] RCIA 127.
[53] RCIA 548.

> The scrutinies, which are . . . reinforced by an exorcism, are rites for self-searching and repentance. . . . These rites, therefore, should complete the conversion of the elect and deepen their resolve to hold fast to Christ and to carry out their decision to love God above all.[54]

However, baptized candidates should already be converted, and they should already possess a deep resolve to hold fast to Christ and to love God above all. Those are qualities of their baptismal status. At some point in their formation, there should no longer be any difference between a "catechized" and an "uncatechized" candidate. All candidates should be catechized and ready for the sacraments. No one is perfect, so a penitential rite seemed appropriate for candidates. Its introduction, however, makes sense only if the candidates were uncatechized and if their reception will take place at Easter:

> This penitential rite can serve to mark the Lenten purification of baptized but previously uncatechized adults. . . . It is held within a celebration of the word of God as a kind of scrutiny, similar to the scrutinies for catechumens.
>
> Because the penitential rite normally belongs to the period of final preparation for the sacraments, its celebration presumes that the candidates are approaching the maturity of faith and understanding requisite for fuller life in the community.[55]

Many baptized candidates approaching the full communion of the Catholic Church have long held "maturity of faith and understanding." This rite was not designed for them. However, the introduction also says, "This penitential rite may also help to prepare the candidates to celebrate the sacrament of penance."[56] This rite was designed for the Second Sunday of Lent, but another occasion may be chosen if the candidates are to be received at another time of year apart from the Easter Vigil.[57]

[54] RCIA 141.
[55] RCIA 459–60.
[56] RCIA 461.
[57] RCIA 462.

OUTLINE OF THE RITES	
SCRUTINY	PENITENTIAL RITE (SCRUTINY)
Invitation to Silent Prayer	Invitation to Silent Prayer
Intercessions for the Elect	Intercessions for the Candidates
Exorcism	Prayer over the Candidates
Dismissal of the Elect	

After the readings and homily of the Mass, the celebrant invites the candidates forward. The community prays in silence for them, and the candidates kneel or bow their heads for prayer.[58] Intercessions and prayer are made for them, during which the celebrant may impose hands on each of the candidates.[59] Whereas the scrutiny rites include a prayer of exorcism at this point, the penitential rite offers a kind of blessing. For example, "Pour out upon [these candidates] the power of your Spirit, that they may be fearless witnesses to your Gospel and one with us in the communion of love." Or, "May they ever keep safe in all its fullness the gift your love once gave them and your mercy now restores."[60] In the scrutinies, exorcisms presume that the spirit of evil had a stronger hand upon the elect because they were unbaptized. In the penitential rite, the prayers presume that the candidates—because of their baptism—are more responsible for the sin they commit. However, it should not appear that candidates need to be absolved from the sin of heresy, as was formerly the case.

Overall, the structure is identical to the scrutinies. The liturgical gestures are the same. There are subtle but meaningful changes in the texts of the prayers, but many of these will go unnoticed. There is no combined rite. The separation of nearly identical ceremonies by one week was intended to show that candidates are not the same as the elect.

[58] RCIA 468.
[59] RCIA 469–70.
[60] RCIA 470AB.

There are other ceremonies designed for the unbaptized, such as the Presentation of the Creed and the Presentation of the Lord's Prayer. The RCIA permitted these presentations to be made to baptized, uncatechized Catholics if the ceremonies fit the conditions and spirituality of such candidates.[61] The American edition expanded the use of these presentations to all other baptized candidates, provided they were uncatechized. In practice, however, many parishes offer the presentations to catechized candidates as well.

The preparation rites of Holy Saturday morning are prebaptismal.[62] There is no adaptation of them for baptized candidates. However, in practice, some parishes inappropriately celebrate these prebaptismal ceremonies for those who are already baptized.

These were the preliminary rites, then, created for baptized, uncatechized adults. In practice, they have been used for many candidates, regardless their level of catechesis.

The Combined Rite at the Easter Vigil

The American edition also includes a combined rite of reception and baptism for use at the Easter Vigil. It bears an unwieldy title, as all the combined rites do: Celebration at the Easter Vigil of the Sacraments of Initiation and of the Rite of Reception into the Full Communion of the Catholic Church.[63] It appeared in the liturgical book over some objections. As the combined rite was being prepared, the Congregation for Divine Worship denied permission to include it:

> 1. Apart from liturgical reasons, an ecumenical motive for not accepting the innovation was given in a letter to this Dicastery from the Secretariat for Promoting Christian Unity: "The insertion of this rite into the Easter Vigil gives such importance to the event that it may cause surprise and even pain to our fellow Christians and give rise to new difficulties."

[61] RCIA 407. This paragraph also mentions a presentation of a book of the gospels, an option that was eliminated before the final version of the catechumenate rites was approved. A remnant of it remains in the Rite of Acceptance, when the new catechumens are invited into the church to share the table of God's word (RCIA 60), and when "the celebrant speaks to them briefly, helping them to understand the dignity of God's word" (RCIA 61).

[62] RCIA 185–205.

[63] RCIA 562–94.

2. The following liturgical reasons cannot be ignored since the Easter Vigil has its own proper character:

    i. It is not opportune to introduce new elements into the rite of baptism and confirmation. Care must be taken to distinguish between catechumens and converts [sic].

    ii. The *Ordo Initiationis Christianæ Adultorum* provides a proper rite in which the following points are to be noted:

        a. the Mass for Christian Unity can be celebrated;

        b. the recitation of the Nicene-Constantinopolitan Creed is prescribed as part of the rite of reception (n. 15);

        c. the rite of admission should immediately follow the homily.

    iii. The third paragraph of the *Prænotanda* states that "any appearance of triumphalism should be carefully avoided. . . . Often it will be preferable to celebrate the Mass with only a few relatives and friends." It follows then that there can be no change in our decision of 20 June 1986 [Letter of Virgil Noe, Secretary CDW to John Page, Executive Secretary of ICEL, 20 June 1986, CDW Prot. 735/86], which stated that the rite of reception into the full communion of the Catholic Church could not be celebrated during the Easter Vigil.[64]

Because of ecumenical sensitivity, the combined rite for the Easter Vigil was being discouraged. A combined rite had been discussed and rejected by the study group drafting the rite of reception. When the same idea arose in the United States after the *editio typica* was published, two Roman congregations stood by the decision.

In the end, though, the combined rites for the Easter Vigil were approved. People were already celebrating them, so the Congregation thought it was advisable to approve a liturgy explaining how it should be done. Still, the Secretariat for Promoting Christian Unity as well as the Congregation for Divine Worship were concerned

[64] Letter of Virgil Noe, Secretary CDW to Bishop Doyle, 1 September 1986, CDW prot. 432/86. This was confirmed in another letter of Noe to Bishop Malone, 18 October 1986, CDW prot. 898/86. Archives of the Bishops' Committee on the Liturgy, National Conference of Catholic Bishops (U.S.A.). (Cited in Sieverding, *Ordo admissionis*, 279–280.)

. . . not to promote anything that would seem to deny the validity of the baptism of Christians already baptized in their own Churches. . . . [This lead to the] impression that the proposal [of the combined rite] was an attempt to bring closer together the baptism of those never before baptized and those being received into Catholic Communion.

[As is now clear] the fundamental fact is the widespread and established RCIA programme which both in its catechumenate and in its practice of Christian initiation at Easter grouped together indiscriminately all those to be received into Catholic Communion but not needing to be baptized.

In this case the proposed new rite appears in a different light, i.e., as making a distinction which badly needs to be made. [The combined rite then is seen as a solution proposed] to remedy a situation that will not otherwise be easily improved.[65]

An unofficial letter states that the Secretariat's objection was lifted because it was realized that "it is an amelioration of an unsatisfactory situation and not a step in an undesirable direction."[66]

The Congregation for Divine Worship approved the combined rites for the United States, as well as for other conferences that requested them, on condition that they be placed in an appendix. The other combined rites, unique to the United States, were given a conditional confirmation in order not to delay publication.[67]

The combined rite takes place after the Liturgy of the Word at the Easter Vigil. As requested by the Congregation for Divine Worship, the ritual appears in the appendix of the *Rite of Christian Initiation of Adults*.

[65] Letter of Basil Meeking, Under-Secretary, Secretariat for Promoting Christian Unity to John Hotchkin, Executive Director of the Bishop's Committee for Ecumenical and Interreligious Affairs, NCCB (U.S.A.), 22 August 1986, SPCU prot. 4132/86/D. Archives of the Bishops' Committee on the Liturgy, National Conference of Catholic Bishops (U.S.A.). (Cited in Sieverding, *Ordo admissionis*, 280.)

[66] Letter of Meeking to Hotchkin, 30 October 1986. Archives of the Bishops' Committee on the Liturgy, National Conference of Catholic Bishops (U.S.A.). (Cited in Sieverding, *Ordo admissionis*, 280.)

[67] Letter of Augustin Mayer, Cardinal Prefect, CDW to Archbishop May, President of the NCCB, 19 February 1988, CDW prot. 1192/86. Archives of the Bishops' Committee on the Liturgy, National Conference of Catholic Bishops (U.S.A.). (Cited in Sieverding, *Ordo admissionis*, 280.)

In some parishes, baptized uncatechized Catholics have completed their preparation for confirmation and/or First Communion. The bishop is the ordinary minister of confirmation for these Catholics, but in some dioceses he gives the faculty to confirm to a priest at the parish. This further complicates the rites and makes the meaning of confirmation more difficult to interpret.

OUTLINE OF THE RITES	
CELEBRATION OF THE SACRAMENTS OF INITIATION (EASTER VIGIL)	CELEBRATION AT THE EASTER VIGIL OF THE SACRAMENTS OF INITIATION AND OF THE RITE OF RECEPTION INTO THE FULL COMMUNION OF THE CATHOLIC CHURCH
CELEBRATION OF BAPTISM	CELEBRATION OF BAPTISM
	RENEWAL OF BAPTISMAL PROMISES
	CELEBRATION OF RECEPTION
CELEBRATION OF CONFIRMATION	CELEBRATION OF CONFIRMATION
RENEWAL OF BAPTISMAL PROMISES	

Those to be received into full communion and their sponsors "should take places apart from the elect."[68] The liturgy of baptism is celebrated in its entirety, through the presentation of a lighted candle. A change occurs at that point. If baptisms were being celebrated *without* the rite of reception, the newly baptized would be confirmed immediately.[69] Then the entire community would renew its baptismal promises, and all would be sprinkled with baptismal water.[70] The Liturgy of the Eucharist would begin as usual with the general inter-

[68] RCIA 586.
[69] RCIA 231–35.
[70] RCIA 235–40.

cessions, and continue until it would bring the Easter Vigil to its close. The original intent was to place confirmation in closest proximity to baptism:

> The conjunction of the two celebrations signifies the unity of the paschal mystery, the close link between the mission of the Son and the outpouring of the Holy Spirit, and the connection between the two sacraments through which the Son and the Holy Spirit come with the Father to those who are baptized.[71]

In the Vigil liturgy without the rite of reception, the faithful do not renew their baptismal promises until after the unbroken celebration of baptism and confirmation. At that point, the newly baptized take their places with the entire assembly for the renewal of promises.[72] The newly baptized make this "renewal," even though they have just made their baptismal promises for the first time.

In the combined rite, the liturgy interrupts this sequence and inserts the rite of reception after the presentation of the baptismal candle and before confirmation. The newly baptized wait to be confirmed. In fact, before they are confirmed they renew their baptismal promises with the candidates for reception and with the entire congregation—even earlier than they do in the liturgy without the rite of reception.[73] "All the people" are sprinkled with baptismal water, including those who were just baptized but are not yet confirmed.[74]

The rite of reception begins with the invitation of the celebrant.[75] The candidates are asked to make their profession of faith, "I believe and profess all that the holy Catholic Church believes, teaches, and proclaims to be revealed by God." They may do so as a group. When this rite is celebrated apart from the Easter Vigil, this statement comes immediately after the recitation of the Creed, linking it to the apostolic faith. But at the Easter Vigil, the Creed is replaced by the renewal of promises, and the candidates' profession of Catholic faith is deferred until after all have been sprinkled with water and until after the celebrant has invited them forward. It is left hanging by itself without a

---

[71] RCIA 215.
[72] RCIA 236.
[73] RCIA 580.
[74] RCIA 583.
[75] RCIA 584.

sequential link to the Creed.[76] The celebrant then recites the act of reception for them one by one: "N., the Lord receives you into the Catholic Church."[77]

Confirmation comes at this point,[78] which is the normal sequence in the rite of reception, but is somewhat delayed for the newly baptized. Both groups are confirmed together. No distinctions are made between the newly baptized, who celebrate confirmation as a part of baptismal initiation, and the newly received, who celebrate it as a perfecting of their baptismal status in preparation for the Eucharist.

The meaning of communion is slightly different for the two groups—the newly baptized receive it as the completion of their single initiation ceremony, whereas the others are completing their reception into the full communion of the Catholic Church. The celebrant is supposed to note this distinction in a remark before communion:

> Before saying "This is the Lamb of God," the celebrant may briefly remind the neophytes of the preeminence of the eucharist, which is the climax of their initiation and the center of the whole Christian life. He may also mention that for those received into full communion this first full sharing with the Catholic community in eucharistic communion is the high point of their reception.[79]

So, although some distinctions are made at the Easter Vigil between those to be baptized and those to be received, each makes some compromises for the other, and both are confirmed and share their First Communion together.

On the whole, the English translation of the Rite of Christian Initiation of Adults is a wonderful achievement of faithfulness and creativity. However, in the interest of offering baptized candidates more from the church's store of liturgical worship, the RCIA eliminated many of the sharp distinctions between baptized candidates and catechumens.

[76] RCIA 585.
[77] RCIA 586.
[78] RCIA 587.
[79] RCIA 594.

Part III

The Journey to Fullness

Chapter 6

Siblings

The parents of the rite of reception are the historical development of the liturgical rite and the ecumenical movement. The same parents gave birth to other children: several other churches that also developed rites for baptized Christians who were transferring from one communion to another. A survey of their ritual texts reveals their theology of baptism, church, and communion. This theology differs from the Catholic perspective. It creates a background against which the Catholic theology of the rite of reception can be seen in relief.

While some churches have developed formal rites for reception, many Christian groups receive new members without a published liturgical rite. Fundamentalist and evangelical Christians, for example, may welcome new members with a combination of testimony, preaching, song, and proclamation. They sometimes receive other baptized Christians by baptizing them because they insist on "believer's baptism."

This survey is limited to published ritual texts. It is enlightening as far as it goes, but the complete context is much broader than this chapter indicates. Christians in one denomination receive Christians from another in a wide variety of ways.

THE ANGLICAN COMMUNION

The Anglican communion exemplifies a unified approach to receiving baptized Christians, with some local variations in different parts of the world. The Episcopal Church adopted a change in language and liturgical form when receiving someone previously baptized. Marion Hatchett explains,

> The form designed for use with the laying on of hands for a person baptized within another tradition who wishes to affiliate with the

Episcopal Church incorporates a recognition of membership in the church which is described in the Offices of Instruction of the 1928 Book and in the Catechism of this edition (p. 854) as "the Body of which Jesus Christ is the Head and of which all baptized persons are members."[1]

Hatchett believes this form grew from those used by the Church of England for "Protestants" or "Converted Papists" in the late seventeenth or early eighteenth centuries.

The person is described as one "who wishes to affiliate." The ceremony involves "a recognition of membership" in the Body of Christ. The commentary says the form may be compared with the Roman rite of reception, but there are differences. In the Roman rite, the person may wish to affiliate, but the Roman Church sees it as something more—a completion of baptism. The ceremony of the Episcopal Church is described in the Book of Common Prayer under the heading, "Confirmation with forms for Reception and for Reaffirmation of Baptismal Vows."[2]

The bishop presides. The ceremony has to do with a "public affirmation" of faith and "commitment to the responsibilities" of baptism for those who were baptized but who had never received handlaying from a bishop. It does not add anything to one's baptism. The ceremony is included in the rite of confirmation, which consequently has several forms. When a baptized person is to be affiliated with the Episcopal Church, the following conversation ensues:

> *Presenters:* I present *these persons* to be received into this Communion.
>
> *The Bishop asks the candidates:* Do you reaffirm your renunciation of evil?
>
> *Candidate:* I do.
>
> *Bishop:* Do you renew your commitment to Jesus Christ?
>
> *Candidate:* I do, and with God's grace I will follow him as my Savior and Lord.[3]

[1] Marion J. Hatchett, *Commentary on the American Prayer Book* (New York: Seabury Press, 1981) 282–83.

[2] *The Book of Common Prayer and Administration of the Sacraments and Other Rites and Ceremonies of the Church Together with the Psalter or Psalms of David According to the use of the Episcopal Church* (New York: Church Publishing Incorporated, 1979) 413.

[3] Ibid., 415.

As part of the ceremony of reception, the bishop makes this statement:

> N., we recognize you as a member of the one holy catholic and apostolic Church and we receive you into the fellowship of this Communion. God, the Father, Son, and Holy Spirit, bless, preserve, and keep you. **Amen.**[4]

In the Roman Catholic rite, the priest says, "The Lord Jesus receives you into the Catholic Church." In the Episcopal Church, the bishop says, "we recognize you as a member."

In Australia, the ceremony is separated from the various forms of confirmation under the title, "Reception into Communicant Membership."[5] The ceremony begins when the priest or a lay sponsor presents the candidate to the bishop:

> 2. *The bishop says to the candidate.*
>
> Do you stand by the Christian confession and commitment made at your baptism?
>
> **I do.**
>
> Do you desire to be admitted into communicant membership of the Anglican Church of Australia and accept her doctrine and order?
>
> **I do.**
>
> 3. *The bishop welcomes the person in these words, taking him/her by the hand.*
>
> We recognize you as a baptized and communicant member of the Christian Church.
>
> The congregation responds
>
> **We receive and welcome you into the communion of the Anglican Church.**[6]

---

[4] Ibid., 418.

[5] *A Prayer Book for Australia* for use together with *The Book of Common Prayer* (1662) and *An Australian Prayer Book* (1978) (Alexandria: Broughton Books, 1995) 95.

[6] Ibid., 96–97.

Next the bishop prays that the Holy Spirit will strengthen the candidate, who then kneels for handlaying by the bishop. The bishop also prays that the Spirit will direct and uphold the candidate in the service of Christ and the fellowship of the church.

The ritual receives one who was formerly a communicant member of one church into the membership of the Anglican Church of Australia. One's membership in the Body of Christ and one's baptismal status is not affected. The bishop and the community receive and welcome the new member. The rite may be inserted in ceremonies of baptism, confirmation, or communion.

In the Anglican Church a bishop must administer this rite. His ministry expresses the unity of the Body of Christ. The Standing Liturgical Commission and the Theological and Prayer Book Committees of the House of Bishops explains that one bishop represents the worldwide episcopate. He appropriately blesses with handlaying and recommissions the candidate to Christian service.[7]

Although Anglicans have consistently recognized the baptism of other Christian bodies, they did not always recognize confirmations, even those performed by bishops in the Catholic Church, which "contain no public affirmation of faith."[8] It is not clear why the author did not recognize the renewal of baptismal promises in the Catholic confirmation rite as a "public affirmation of faith." Nonetheless, his position elucidates the discrepancy over the meaning of confirmation in the two church bodies—for Catholics the main point is the gift of the Holy Spirit, rather than a public statement.

In practice, a decision to recognize the confirmation of other churches is made locally. The idea is "to enable the public reception into the communicant life of the Church of England of those who are judged to be episcopally confirmed," including Catholics and the Nordic Churches of the Porvoo Agreement, who practice a presbyteral confirmation without chrism.[9]

The ritual evolved as it has in the Catholic tradition, both in regard to the suitability of certain candidates and to the structure of the rite. For example, the prayer for the candidates had already appeared in similar rites.

---

[7] See Hatchett, *Commentary on the American Prayer Book*, 272.

[8] Ibid.

[9] *Common Worship: Initiation Services* (London: Church House Publishing, 1998) 203.

The Affirmation candidates now have a prayer said over them. This is also found in the JLG [Joint Liturgical Group of Great Britain] rite, *Confirmation and Re-affirmation of Baptismal Faith* (1997). A similar prayer is also to be found in the 1989 New Zealand Prayer Book. The prayer for those being received is a modification of a similar text found in the JLG rite. The words of reception are also similar to those in the 1979 American *BCP* [*Book of Common Prayer*] and the Canadian *BAS* [*Book of Alternative Services of the Anglican Church of Canada*, 1985].[10]

The ceremony is fairly simple. However, efforts have been under-way to expand it by incorporating a variety of optional rites as appear in the United States edition of the Roman Catholic *Rite of Christian Initiation of Adults*. When the Episcopal Church in the United States started working with the catechumenate, it included the case of baptized persons as well. "The 1988 General Convention in Detroit called for implementation of the adult catechumenate and parallel rites for the baptized."[11]

Originally, the Catechumenate was developed specifically—and solely—for people seeking baptism. Today, many people who are already baptized—often as infants—seek further preparation for an active, committed role in the church. . . . Limitations of human "resources" and of space in most congregations have led many to look for ways to include both unbaptized and baptized seekers in one group. When the two groups meet as one, however, there should still be a distinction made between the needs and goals of the two groups and in the choice of rites to accompany their journeys.[12]

These rites for baptized seekers include The Welcoming of Baptized Christians into a Community, in which they sign the parish register; The Calling of the Baptized to Continuing Conversion, in which they

---

[10] Simon Jones and Phillip Tovey, "Initiation Services," in *A Companion to Common Worship*, ed. Paul Bradshaw, vol. I, Alcuin Club Collections 78 (London: SPCK, 2001) 176.

[11] *The Catechumenal Process: Adult Initiation & Formation for Christian Life and Ministry, a Resource for Dioceses and Congregations*, Offices of Evangelism Ministries, The Episcopal Church Center (New York: Church Hymnal Corporation, 1990) [v].

[12] Ibid., x.

receive and help impose ashes; and the Maundy Thursday Rite, in which they receive and share in foot-washing.[13] Maundy Thursday may also include a reconciliation rite for all participants, though one that omits the confession of particular sins.[14] This last rite carries peculiar resonances with an old custom of reconciling penitents on that day. Baptized Christians seeking new membership should not be confused with public sinners.

THE CHURCH OF SOUTH INDIA

The Church of South India includes among its rites for Christian Initiation a ceremony called "The Reception of Members from Other Churches." The minister may be a presbyter. If the newcomers are "baptized and communicant members in good standing of Churches in communion with the Church of South India," they are to bring letters of recommendation from a person with some responsibility in their former church. When the minister is satisfied that all is in order, their names are read out during public worship. The minister says, "We bid you welcome to the fellowship of this Church, in the name of the Father, and of the Son, and of the Holy Spirit."[15]

However, if the newcomers are baptized communicant members from a church not in communion with the Church of South India, a more involved procedure takes place. It permits a presbyter to lead the rite, perhaps due to the scarcity of bishops.

Prior to the ceremony the presbyter investigates the motives of the candidates and makes a report to the Pastorate Committee and the bishop. The ritual preferably takes place at a celebration of the Lord's Supper.

The presbyter introduces the ceremony with a prayer. Then he asks the candidates if they "desire to be admitted into the Church of South India as a communicant member," if they accept the teachings and discipline of the church, and if they will remain faithful to that teaching. When the candidates answer affirmatively, the presbyter leads a prayer for mercy and the Lord's Prayer. Then he offers an oration that includes this petition:

---

[13] Ibid., 145–46.

[14] Ibid., 99; cf. *Book of Common Prayer*, 450.

[15] *The Book of Common Worship: The Church of South India* (London, New York, Madras: Oxford University Press, 1963) xxi.

> Grant to thy *servant* the continued aid of thy Holy Spirit, that
> abiding with us in the fellowship of thy holy Church, *he* may
> remain faithful in thy service and obtain thy promises.

While extending the right hand, the presbyter says,

> We admit you into the fellowship of the Church of South India,
> in the name of the Father, and of the Son, and of the Holy Spirit.
> **Amen.**

He also prays that God will make the candidates perfect and
strengthen them.[16]

The Church of South India stresses the importance of an inquiry
into the motives and readiness of the new members. This status is
formalized in ritual questions. The prayer for perseverance presumes
that the Holy Spirit already abides in the new members by reason of
their baptism, and that they have been faithful in God's service. This
ritual prays for strengthening on the occasion of one's transferring
membership. The statement of reception is brief, a simple declaration
of membership and friendship. It presumes that baptism brings one
into the church, and this step indicates in which manifestation of the
church the person will be a member.

THE METHODIST CHURCH IN ENGLAND

The Methodist Church in England outlines a service for The Reception of Christians of Other Communions into the Membership of the
Methodist Church.[17] It expresses its purpose as helping those who
were members of other communions within the Church of Christ to
become members of the Methodist Church, another exemplar of the
same Church of Christ to which all the baptized belong. In this case,
the reception happens on the strength of the person's desire, even
before questions of commitment are addressed.

The minister asks them, "Do you now wish to be *members* of the
Methodist Church?" They answer affirmatively. The minister says,

---

[16] Ibid., xxi–xxiii.

[17] *The Methodist Worship Book* (Peterborough, England: Methodist Publishing
House, 1999) 353–54.

"*N and N (N)*, we receive and welcome you as *members* of the Methodist Church and of the church in this place." The minister adds words of blessing and extends the hand of fellowship.

This essentially completes the reception of the new members. The minister continues with further questions:

> Do you commit yourself with us to the Christian life of worship and service, and to be open to the renewing power of God?

> Will you continue to seek the strength of God's Spirit as you follow Jesus Christ in your daily life?

> Will you witness, by word and deed, to the Good News of God in Christ, and so bring glory to God?

The new members answer affirmatively. Finally, the minister asks all the members if they will build each other up in love. They agree, and the service continues.[18]

THE UNITED METHODIST CHURCH

The United Methodist Church in the United States offers a similar service. It is not to be confused with the preparation of the unbaptized. In general "the congregation and its leaders will affirm their baptism and welcome their participation as members of the body of Christ." However, they may be included with small formational groups of the unbaptized. Large groups are best kept separate. Services for candidates for baptism are not appropriate for those already baptized.[19]

There is also a Celebration of Reconciliation on Holy Thursday[20] and an Affirmation of the Baptismal Covenant at the Easter Vigil,[21] but these are for those who are returning to the baptismal covenant after having been away from it for a while, not explicitly for one transferring from one Christian church to another.[22]

---

[18] Ibid.

[19] Daniel T. Benedict Jr., *Come to the Waters: Baptism & Our Ministry of Welcoming Seekers and Making Disciples* (Nashville: Discipleship Resources, 1996) 68.

[20] Ibid., 148–50.

[21] Ibid., 142.

[22] Cf. ibid., 138.

The pertinent service concerns those baptized in other churches who wish to become Methodists. Two versions are offered.[23] "The Baptismal Covenant I" embraces a number of possible rituals: holy baptism, confirmation, reaffirmation of faith, reception into the United Methodist Church, and reception into a local congregation. If someone is to be received, a representative of the congregation presents the candidates with this statement: "I present Name(s) who come(s) to this congregation from the _____ Church."[24] The candidates renounce sin and profess faith, and the congregation expresses its willingness to support them.[25] All reaffirm their faith with the Apostles' Creed.[26] Then comes reception for those transferring their membership into the United Methodist Church. The pastor asks,

> As members of Christ's universal Church,
> Will you be loyal to The United Methodist Church,
> And do all in your power to strengthen its ministries?[27]

After they agree, the pastor commends those received to the care of the congregation and addresses them with these words: "The God of all grace, who has called us to eternal glory in Christ, establish you and strengthen you by the power of the Holy Spirit, that you may live in grace and peace."[28]

"The Baptismal Covenant III" also includes a service of reception into the United Methodist Church for those who are "members of other communions in Christ's holy Church." He asks those who have transferred and those who have just professed their faith through baptism or confirmation if they will be loyal to the United Methodist Church with prayers, presence, gifts, and service. They agree.[29]

The pastor commends the new members to the congregation, which recognizes them as "members of Christ's holy Church" and welcomes them to their company.[30]

---

[23] *The United Methodist Book of Worship* (Nashville: United Methodist Publishing House, 1992) 86–94, 106–10.

[24] Ibid., 87.

[25] Ibid., 88–89.

[26] Ibid., 89–90.

[27] Ibid., 93.

[28] Ibid., 94.

[29] Ibid., 109.

[30] Ibid., 109–10.

These services continue to undergo reflection:

> Methodism, with its roots as a Society within the established
> Church, has retained up till now the language of 'full member-
> ship.' This jars somewhat with the theological principle that it is
> baptism that confers (full!) membership of Christ's Church, and a
> Faith and Order Working Party on ecclesiology is currently looking
> at this issue.[31]

THE UNITED CHURCH OF CHRIST

When the United Church of Christ receives previously baptized
people into membership, it uses its Order for Reception of Members:
Affirmation of Baptism.[32] The introduction distinguishes between
those uniting by a ceremony of reaffirmation and those doing so with
a letter of transfer or other certification. If the ceremony is to be
followed, appropriate local leaders first confirm the candidates' level
of instruction and desire. If certificates are obtained, the leaders verify
that they are in order.[33]

Some new members, therefore, are simply recognized with no
further ceremony attached. However, if a ceremony is to happen,
it begins when a leader invites forward those who wish to affirm their
baptism by uniting with the local household of faith. Names are read,
letters of transfer may be presented, and the leader gives an
introduction.[34]

After this come sentences from Scripture, questions of the candidates,
and an affirmation of faith.[35] The pastor affirms that the candidates are
already "one with us in the body of Christ, the church," and asks if
they will share in worship and enlist in the church's work for the community and the world. When the candidates make this promise, they
are welcomed and received by the people, who say:

---

[31] David Kennedy and Phillip Tovey, *Methodist and United Reformed Church
Worship: Baptism and Communion in Two 'Free' Churches*, Grove Worship Series
No. 120 (Bramcote, Nottingham: Grove Books Limited, 1992) 10.

[32] *Book of Worship: United Church of Christ* (New York: United Church of
Christ Office for Church Life and Leadership, 1986) 157–65.

[33] Ibid., 157–58.

[34] Ibid., 159.

[35] Ibid., 162.

We welcome you with joy in the common life of this church. We promise you our friendship and prayers as we share the hopes and labors of the church of Jesus Christ. By the power of the Holy Spirit may we continue to grow together in God's knowledge and love and be witnesses of our risen Savior.[36]

The pastor and representatives may then greet the new members, welcoming them to the local church with "the hand of Christian love."[37] The final prayer may take one of three forms. The prayers summarize what is happening to the individual new members as well as to the community. The first form thanks God for sending the new members "that we may work together in serving the needs of others." The second prays that the Holy Spirit may ever be with the new members and lead them "in the knowledge and obedience of your Word." The third thanks God for all gathered in the local church and rejoices that the numbers have increased: "Together may we live in the spirit, building one another up in love, sharing in the life and worship of the church, and serving the world for the sake of Jesus Christ."[38]

The ceremony is primarily an affirmation of baptism and the unity of the church. Although a particular membership is being established, that is not the focus. Rather, the new members affirm their baptism and place their gifts at the service of Jesus Christ. Members of the local church express welcome, and the pastor promises friendship and prayer on behalf of the people. The final prayers are as much for the entire community as they are for the individuals joining it.

THE EVANGELICAL LUTHERAN CHURCH IN AMERICA

The Evangelical Lutheran Church in America bundles three services together: affirmation of baptism, confirmation, and restoration to membership. The first includes the reception of baptized Christians to membership. The second primarily concerns Lutherans baptized as infants, and the last those who have been away from the church for some time.[39] A commentary explains that the affirmation of baptism serves three occasions:

---

[36] Ibid., 163.

[37] Ibid., 163–65.

[38] Ibid., 164–65.

[39] *Lutheran Book of Worship* (Minneapolis and Philadelphia: Augsburg Publishing House and Board of Publication, Lutheran Church in America, 1982) 198–201.

. . . confirmation (understood as the completion of a period of
instruction in the Christian faith as confessed in the teachings of
the Lutheran Church); reception of Christians from other denomi-
nations into membership in the Lutheran Church through reception
into a local congregation; and restoration of the lapsed to active
participation in the life of the church.[40]

The *Lutheran Book of Worship* says that other Christians become
members of the Lutheran Church through reception into a particular
congregation. "In Baptism they were made Christians; now they
become members of the Lutheran Church."[41]

The ceremony will identify the new members as Lutherans, while
recognizing that their status as Christians has not changed. The commentary explains:

> In each of the three uses, the candidates are understood by virtue
> of their baptism already to be members of the church, and this rite
> adds nothing to that enduring foundation and well-spring of the
> Christian life. Holy Baptism is necessary; this service is not.[42]

The ceremony begins when a representative of the local congregation presents those who desire to make public affirmation of their baptism. Their names are read, and the pastor says, "We rejoice to receive
you, members of the one holy catholic and apostolic Church, into our
fellowship in the Gospel.[43]

Thus they are recognized as members of the one church, and are
received into Lutheran "fellowship in the Gospel." Then all make the
profession of faith in a question and answer form. Prayers are offered.
A minister asks the new members if they intend to continue to hear
God's word, share the supper, proclaim the good news, serve others,
and strive for justice and peace. Each person agrees and asks God's
help.

---

[40] Philip H. Pfatteicher, *Commentary on the Lutheran Book of Worship: Lutheran
Liturgy in Its Ecumenical Context* (Minneapolis: Augsburg Fortress, 1990) 68.

[41] *Lutheran Book of Worship*, 198.

[42] Pfatteicher, *Commentary on the Lutheran Book of Worship*, 68.

[43] *Lutheran Book of Worship*, 198.

As the candidates kneel, the pastor prays for them. "Continue to strengthen them with the Holy Spirit," the pastor says, while asking God to increase the gifts of the spirit.[44]

Throughout, the ceremony challenges the individuals to continue their membership in the one Church, while doing so now as Lutherans. New members reaffirm their baptism and its expectations. The pastor prays that the Spirit will "continue" to strengthen them. A commentary explains that those being received are already members of the church and are moving from one local assembly to another.[45]

An early manual on this liturgy summarizes the procedure and meaning of the ritual this way:

> A lay leader of the congregation presents those from other denominations who are to be received into membership in the Lutheran Church. The pastor's welcome makes clear that they are already by Baptism members of the "One Holy, Catholic, and Apostolic Church" and now are to become more particularly members of the Lutheran family.[46]

THE UNITED REFORMED CHURCH

The United Reformed Church in the United Kingdom also offers a service called Reception of Members from Other Churches.[47] After the ceremony is introduced, the leader asks for the affirmation that those presenting themselves will live as faithful members of their new community. The leader asks them to confess their faith and trust in God, to trust in God's grace, to worship, and to share the witness of the church. When the new members say, "I do," the minister makes a gesture of welcome and says, "In the name of the Lord Jesus Christ, welcome." Then the congregation may make a statement:

> In the name of Christ we welcome you. May we grow together in unity, and be built up into the body of Christ in love, to the glory of God, Father, Son, and Holy Spirit, now and for ever. Amen.[48]

[44] Ibid., 201.

[45] Pfatteicher, *Commentary on the Lutheran Book of Worship*, 72.

[46] Philip H. Pfatteicher and Carlos R. Messerli, *Manual on the Liturgy: Lutheran Book of Worship* (Minneapolis: Augsburg Publishing House, 1979) 343.

[47] *Service Book: The United Reformed Church in the United Kingdom* (Oxford: Oxford University Press, 1989) 47–48.

[48] Ibid.

In this ceremony, the ones being received are asked several questions about their belief and promise to be faithful to the Christian responsibilities of worship, living in fellowship, and sharing witness. A sign of welcome is offered with a simple statement. The congregation adds its welcome and its hope for growing together. The ritual, called "reception," is very much a welcome of those who have publicly stated their intention to be members.

THE DISCIPLES OF CHRIST

The Disciples of Christ offer confirmation "for those baptized at some time in the past who come to make their own confession of Christian faith and enter into the full privileges and responsibilities of membership in Christ's church."[49] But the same resource includes a specific recognition of those who are becoming new members. The congregation makes this recognition in a common statement:

> Reaffirming our own faith in Jesus the Christ, we gladly welcome you into this community of faith, enfolding you with our love and committing ourselves to your care.

> In the power of God's Spirit let us mutually encourage each other to trust God and strengthen one another to serve others, that Christ's church may in all things stand faithful.

> +

The congregation may also make this statement:

> We welcome you with joy in the common life of this church. We promise you our friendship and prayers as we share the hopes and labors of the church of Jesus Christ. By the power of the Holy Spirit may we continue to grow together in God's knowledge and love and be witnesses of our risen Savior.[50]

Little is demanded of those wishing to be known as Disciples of Christ. The local church trusts their personal discernment. Their act of transfer is noted by the congregation, which expresses its desire to welcome the newcomers and commit themselves to their care.

[49] *Chalice Worship*, compiled and edited by Colbert S. Cartwright and O. I. Cricket Harrison (St. Louis: Chalice Press, 1997) 32–33.
[50] Ibid., 214–15.

THE PRESBYTERIAN CHURCH (USA)

The Presbyterian Church (USA) has a Reaffirmation of the Baptismal Covenant for Those Uniting with a Congregation.[51] This service is offered to Presbyterian congregations as a guide for their use; it may be adapted significantly. It makes these distinctions among those who are joining the congregation: Some baptized persons are received by a letter of transfer; others are received on reaffirmation of faith; still others have ceased membership and are restored through reaffirmation of faith.[52]

The ceremony takes place at the baptismal font or pool, and an elder presents the new members to the people, acknowledging the unity they already share as members of the one holy catholic church.[53]

Scripture is read, and the new members make a profession of faith. They renounce evil and profess their faith with the community; for example, in the Creed. A minister asks the new members if they will be faithful in worship and service. They say they will, with God's help.[54]

The minister offers a specific prayer for those who are transferring from one Christian church to another. It acknowledges that God has chosen the new members and prays that all may live in the Spirit. It includes these words: "We thank you for choosing to add to our number brothers and sisters in faith. Together, may we live in your Spirit, and so love one another, that we may have the mind of Jesus."[55]

Some optional rituals may be incorporated. The minister may impose hands and may anoint the new members with oil. But the decision to incorporate such actions is left to the minister. The ceremony concludes with signs and words of welcome and peace.[56]

Thus, the ceremony combines elements of intention and welcome. The new members state their intention to be faithful to their baptismal commitment, and the community extends its welcome.

---

[51] *Book of Common Worship*, prepared by The Theology and Worship Ministry Unit for the Presbyterian Church (USA) and the Cumberland Presbyterian Church (Louisville: Westminster/John Knox Press, 1993) 455–62.

[52] Ibid., 455.

[53] Ibid., 456.

[54] Ibid., 460.

[55] Ibid., 461.

[56] Ibid., 462.

THE UNITED CHURCH OF CANADA

The United Church of Canada offers An Order for The Welcoming of Members from Other Churches. Prior to the ceremony, the session has made the necessary preparations to present the new members at a public service. After the sermon, the minister welcomes into the congregation "persons who are already members of the church of our Lord Jesus Christ."

The clerk calls the names of the new members and announces that the session has made inquiry about them, "and has admitted them to full membership in this congregation of The United Church of Canada." The minister invites the people to receive the new members. Then he tells the newcomers, "In the name of the Lord Jesus Christ we welcome you to the privileges and responsibilities of membership in this congregation." He admonishes them to live up to the calling of God.

The people pledge their friendship, help, and prayers. The minister says a blessing. "The minister and clerk of session extend to the new members the right hand of Fellowship."[57]

This service sees the United Church of Canada as one denomination of the one church. Questions about the intention of those joining have been resolved before the service begins. The minister welcomes the new members "to the privileges and responsibilities" of membership in this congregation, and charges them to live up to their calling.

COMMON ELEMENTS

Each of these ecclesial bodies has its own interests, and it is not fair to treat them as one unit, but some common elements emerge.

1. The ceremonies acknowledge that one who is already baptized is baptized into the one, holy, catholic, apostolic church.

2. The ceremonies recognize that a person wishes to live out his or her baptism in a new congregation.

3. Some evidence is given—a written testimony from the previous congregation's leadership, a time of testing with church leaders in the new congregation, and/or a public statement of faith and intention.

---

[57] *Service Book for the use of ministers conducting public worship* ([S.I.] Canec Publishing & Supply House, 1986) 232–33.

4. The ceremony takes place in the presence of the new congregation, not in private.

5. A recognized leader of the new congregation presides for the ceremony.

6. The congregation makes some statement or gesture of welcome.

7. The ceremony is fairly simple and straightforward. It is celebrating the personal decision of a new member.

THE HOLY ORTHODOX-CATHOLIC APOSTOLIC CHURCH

For a different kind of example, it is worth examining the 1922 *Service Book of the Holy Orthodox-Catholic Apostolic Church*.[58] There is found The Office for Receiving into the Orthodox Faith Such Persons as Have Not Previously Been Orthodox, but who "have been reared from infancy outside the orthodox church, yet have received valid baptism, in the name of the Father and of the Son, and of the Holy Spirit.[59]

According to John Matusiak, communications director for the Orthodox Church of America, the Hapgood translation is generally used to receive into the church those baptized in a non-Orthodox tradition. Renunciations are not always used when the one being received never really adhered to the beliefs of his or her former tradition. Catholics are often received through a statement of faith and the sacraments of confession and Eucharist. They need not be chrismated:

> There is a small minority of Orthodox Christians, "ultra-traditionalist" in style, who insist on baptizing everyone, even those who had been baptized with the aforementioned formula, although this is not the general practice of the Church.[60]

The liturgy goes through several stages: confession of sins, absolution, profession of faith, reception into Orthodoxy, and anointing with

---

[58] New York: Association Press, 1922. Compiled, translated and arranged from the Old Church-Slavonic Service Books of the Russian Church and collated with the Service Books of the Greek Church by Isabel Florence Hapgood. Hereafter, *Service Book*.

[59] Ibid., 454–63.

[60] John Matusiak, Orthodox Church of America Communications Director, in 7 May 2006 e-mail to author.

chrism. The bishop is the ordinary minister, but he may appoint a priest to lead the rite. It begins at the door of the church where the bishop or priest asks this question: "Wilt thou renounce the errors and false doctrines of the Roman-Latin (or Armenian, or Lutheran, or Reformed) Confession?" The one joining answers, "I will," and expresses the desire to join the Orthodox Church.[61]

The bishop recites a prayer that includes these intentions:

> Remove far from him (her) his (her) former errors, and fill him (her) with the true faith, and hope, and love which are in thee. Enable him (her) to walk in all thy commandments, and to fulfil those things which are well-pleasing unto thee; for if a man do these things, he shall also find life in them.[62]

The bishop says to the convert, "Wherefore renounce now, with all thy heart, thine errors, and false doctrines, and mistakes of judgment, and confess the Orthodox-Catholic Faith." He asks the convert from the Roman-Latin Confession to renounce the double procession of the Holy Spirit, the headship of the Bishop of Rome, the primacy of Peter among the apostles, and the infallibility of the pope. Converts from the Armenian Confession must renounce disbelief in the two natures of Christ. Lutherans renounce disbelief in the real presence of Christ, in five of the sacraments, the reverence due to saints, and prayers for the dead. The Reformed renounce predestination.[63]

The convert recites the creed and makes a lengthy statement of acceptance of truths:

> I accept and confess the Apostolic and Ecclesiastical Canons, established at the Seven Holy Ecumenical and Provincial Councils, and the other traditions of the Holy Orthodox-Catholic Apostolic church of the East, its rules and ordinances; and I likewise will accept and understand Holy Scripture in accordance with the interpretation which the Holy Orthodox-Catholic Church of the East, our Mother, hath held, and doth hold.

> I believe and confess that there are Seven Sacraments of the New Testament, to wit: Baptism, Chrismation, the Eucharist, Confession, the Priesthood, Marriage, and Anointing with Oil, instituted

---

[61] *Service Book*, 454.
[62] Ibid., 455.
[63] Ibid., 455–56.

by the Lord Christ and his Church, to the end that, through their operation and reception, we may receive blessings from on high.

I believe and confess that, in the Divine Liturgy, under the mystical forms of bread and wine, the faithful partake of the true Body and Blood of our Lord Jesus Christ, unto the remission of their sins, and unto life eternal.

I believe and confess that it is proper to reverence and invoke the Saints who reign on high with Christ, according to the interpretation of the Holy Orthodox-Catholic Church of the East; and that their prayers and intercessions avail with the beneficent God unto our salvation: Likewise that it is well-pleasing in the sight of God that we should do homage to their relics glorified through incorruption, as the precious memorials of their virtues.

I acknowledge that the images of our Saviour Christ, and of the Ever-virgin Mother of God, and of other Saints are worthy to be possessed and honoured; not unto idolatry, but that, through contemplation thereof, we may be incited unto piety, and unto emulation of the deeds of the holy persons represented by those images.

I confess that the prayers of the faithful, which are offered up to God for the salvation of those who have departed this life in the faith are favourably received, through the mercy of God.

I believe and confess that power hath been given by our Saviour Christ unto the Holy Orthodox-Catholic Church, to bind and to loose: and that whatsoever, by virtue of that power, is bound or loosed on earth will be bound or loosed in heaven.

I believe and confess that the Foundation, head, and Great High Priest and Chief Shepherd of the Holy Orthodox-Catholic Church is our Lord Jesus Christ: and that Bishops, Pastors and Teachers are appointed by him to rule the Church: and that the Guide and Pilot of this Church is the Holy Spirit.

I confess that this Church is the Bride of Christ, and that therein is true salvation.

I promise true obedience, unto my life's end, to the Most Holy Synod (*if it be in a Diocese, then the Bishop of that Diocese is named*), as the true Pastor of the Orthodox Church, and to the Priests appointed by them.[64]

---

[64] Ibid., 458–60.

The bishop gives the end of his pall (or the priest gives the end of his stole) to the convert, and leads him or her by the right hand into the church, saying,

> Enter thou into the Orthodox Church; and cast away all the errors and false doctrines wherein thou hast dwelt: and honour the Lord God, the Father Almighty, and his Only-begotten Son Jesus Christ, and the Holy Spirit, one true and living God, the holy Trinity, one in Essence and indivisible.[65]

A psalm is sung and the convert kneels before the gospels while the bishop asks God to send the Holy Spirit. He continues with a prayer that includes this petition for the convert: "Illumine his (*her*) heart, O Lord, we humbly beseech thee, with the perfect light of the grace of thy Holy Spirit unto the enlightening of his (*her*) mind in the truth of thy Holy Gospel."[66] The convert stands and says,

> This true faith of the Holy Orthodox-Catholic Church, which I now voluntarily confess and unfeignedly hold, I will firmly maintain and confess whole and in its fullness and integrity, until my last breath, God being my helper; and will teach it and proclaim it, so far as in me lieth; and will strive to fulfil its obligations cheerfully and with joy, preserving my heart in purity and virtue. And in confirmation of this, my true and sincere profession of faith, I now kiss the word and cross of my Saviour. Amen.[67]

The bishop says absolution, including these words: "And I, by [Jesus'] almighty power, given unto me, an unworthy Bishop (*or* Priest), through his holy Apostles and their successors, do pardon and absolve thee, my child (N.), from all thy sins: and do unite thee unto the fellowship of the faithful, and unto the body of Christ's Church: and do communicate thee with the Divine Sacraments of the Church: In the Name of the Father, and of the Son, and of the Holy Spirit Amen."[68]

The convert is then anointed with chrism. This entire complex of rituals demonstrates the Orthodox belief that the convert has been in sin and needs absolution, that previous beliefs must be renounced,

[65] Ibid., 461.
[66] Ibid., 461–62.
[67] Ibid., 462.
[68] Ibid., 463.

that the confession of faith must be made clearly, and that chrismation must happen before communion.

SUMMARY

How does one receive into the church a person with a valid baptism? These sibling churches have resolved the question in different ways. Some do it very simply, on a word of testimony. Others involve a brief ceremony in which the new members reaffirm their baptismal faith. Still others have a lengthier ceremony calling for formal renunciation of a former way of belief.

The Rite of Reception of Baptized Christians into the Full Communion of the Catholic Church bears some similarities in structure to the reception of members in many other churches. The members make a statement of belief, and they are received into union with welcome. But the meaning of this ritual is different for Catholics, who see reception not into just another communion of the Body of Christ, but reception into the full communion, which is evident in the Catholic Church.

Chapter 7

Theological Explorations

ONE BAPTISM, BUT . . .

When a baptized Christian transfers from one body into another, the ritual highlights what the receiving body believes about the interrelationship of baptism, church, and communion. Many Christians believe that all three go together: baptism makes one a member of the church and eligible to share communion. The Catholic Church nuances this differently.

The World Council of Churches explained its interpretation of eucharistic communion:

> The eucharistic communion with Christ who nourishes the life of the Church is at the same time communion within the body of Christ which is the Church. . . . It is in the eucharist that the community of God's people is fully manifested.[1]

A commentary notes,

> Since the earliest days, baptism has been understood as the sacrament by which believers are incorporated into the body of Christ and are endowed with the Holy Spirit. As long as the right of the baptized believers and their ministers to participate in and preside over eucharistic celebration in one church is called into question by those who preside over and are members of other eucharistic congregations, the catholicity of the eucharist is less manifest.[2]

---

[1] *Baptism, Eucharist and Ministry*, Faith and Order Paper No. 111 (Geneva: World Council of Churches, 1982) 19:14.

[2] Ibid., 15.

For many non-Catholic Christians, baptism constitutes complete initiation into the Body of Christ. Transferring from one church to another does not enhance one's baptismal status. When visitors come from other Christian assemblies, even if they do not wish to transfer membership, they are welcome to share communion. For these Christians, communion is the privilege of the baptized, not of denominational membership.

After all, "Confessional identity derives from the particular church into which a person is baptized, and not from the rite itself."[3] One is considered a member of the specific body represented by the minister and church of baptism. But baptism admits one into the Body of Christ.

In the Catholic Church, baptism brings about an incomplete initiation. Those validly baptized in another ecclesial body of the West are still ineligible for communion in the Catholic Church unless their baptism is completed in the rite of reception with confirmation. Those baptized in any Eastern Church are considered to have the same baptismal status as those baptized in the Catholic Church, except that Eastern churches offer all the sacraments of initiation at baptism, whereas the Catholic Church defers confirmation and communion.

This theology of initiation affects the Catholic understanding of Christian unity. If initiation is incomplete, the same can be said of unity. "One can deduce from [*Unitatis redintegratio*] that unity is not found absolutely in baptism since the unity achieved is only an 'imperfect' one and baptism is only a 'point of departure' for full unity."[4] "The documents affirm that the unity achieved in baptism is partial, not that the sacrament is deficient or partial."[5]

But it is hard to separate the Catholic belief that baptism does not immediately admit one to the Eucharist from the charge that Catholics regard baptism as something partial. Even those baptized as infants in the Catholic Church do not complete their sacraments of initiation until confirmation and communion—sacraments celebrated at least seven years, sometimes up to seventy years later. The Code of Canon Law effectively creates a second level of church membership for those who have an incomplete initiation:

[3] Susan K. Wood, "Baptism and the Foundations of Communion," in *Baptism & the Unity of the Church*, eds. Michael Root and Risto Saarinen (Grand Rapids: William B. Eerdmans, 1998) 53.

[4] Ibid., 45.

[5] Ibid., 48.

Those who have not been confirmed are ineligible to enter a seminary [24/2], to be ordained [1033], to enter into the novitiate of a religious community [645/1], and to perform the role of godparent at baptism [874/3] and sponsor at confirmation [893/1]. They are encouraged to receive confirmation before marriage [1065/1]. Children who are baptized cannot be admitted to the eucharist without sufficient knowledge, faith, and devotion [913/1]. Even in danger of death, children who cannot distinguish the body of Christ from ordinary food may not receive the eucharist [913/2].[6]

The existence of two different classes among the baptized is difficult to justify. It calls into question statements about baptism as the fundamental bond of communion and the granting of its eschatological gift.[7] Eugene Brand asks rhetorical questions that make the same point:

Is there any basis either in the New Testament or in the classic Tradition of the church for two classes of church members? No. On what ground save disciplinary, then, may communion be withheld from baptized persons? Certainly not on ecclesiological grounds, and not on pneumatological or sacramental grounds either.[8]

The Catholic Church is not alone. Others have called into question statements about baptism as the fundamental bond for communion with Christ.

The Orthodox Church has not fully recognized the baptism of other churches. It accepts—without recognizing—the baptisms of the Roman Catholic and Reformation Churches on the principle of "economy," which distinguishes theory from practice. "Economy here means that in theory the Orthodox Church has not fully accepted the baptisms of other churches to be the baptism of the early church, but in practice accepts it so that it does not baptize those who come from these

---

[6] Paul Turner, "The Double Meaning of 'Initiation' in Theological Expression," in "*Imaginer la théologie catholique*", *Permanence et transformations de la foi en attendant Jésus-Christ: Mélanges offerts à Ghislain Lafont*, ed. Jeremy Driscoll, Studia Anselmiana 129 (Rome: Centro Studi Sant' Anselmo: 2000) 496.

[7] [Michael Root and Risto Saarinen], "Baptism and the Unity of the Church: A Study Paper," in *Baptism & the Unity of the Church*, 29.

[8] Eugene L. Brand, "The Lima Text as a Standard for Current Understandings and Practice of Baptism," in *Studia Liturgica* 16 (1986) 50.

churches into the Orthodox Church."[9] Early Christians included chrismation in the baptismal rites. The Orthodox Church needs to see a more faithful liturgy and a stronger communion among churches in order to consider truly accepting and recognizing non-Orthodox baptism.[10]

Many Catholics would be surprised to hear about the reservations of the Orthodox concerning their baptism. But resistance also shows up in those Christian assemblies that practice believer's baptism. "For various reasons some churches (most prominently but not only those called 'Baptist') believe that the capacity to confess one's own faith is an essential condition for baptism. Only so-called believer's baptism is in fact baptism. The baptism of someone incapable of such confession, e.g., an infant, is simply no baptism."[11]

That there is one baptism is undeniable from the words of Paul to the Ephesians: "[There is] one Lord, one faith, one baptism" (4:5). But there is not one agreement on what those words mean.

TOWARD COMMON GROUND

The World Council of Churches tried to establish a common theological foundation for baptism with its 1982 statement *Baptism, Eucharist and Ministry*. It says that baptism among the various Christian churches is their bond of unity. Moreover, it is the catalyst compelling Christians to a more manifest unity:

> Our common baptism, which unites us to Christ in faith, is thus a basic bond of unity. We are one people and are called to confess and serve one Lord in each place and in all the world. . . . When baptismal unity is realized in one holy, catholic, apostolic Church, a genuine Christian witness can be made to the healing and reconciling love of God. Therefore, our one baptism into Christ constitutes a call to the churches to overcome their divisions and visibly manifest their fellowship.[12]

[9] Merja Merras , "Baptismal Recognition and the Orthodox Churches," in *Baptism & the Unity of the Church*, 144n.

[10] [Michael Root and Risto Saarinen], "Baptism and the Unity of the Church: A Study Paper," 25–26.

[11] Ibid., 26.

[12] *Baptism, Eucharist and Ministry*, 3:3.

In the Catholic Church, the 1983 Code of Canon Law made a somewhat compatible statement: The people of God are those Christians incorporated into Christ through baptism. Indeed, their baptismal unity implies a shared mission. However, the Code also repeated a point from the Second Vatican Council that would become quite significant and controversial, that the church "subsists in" the Catholic Church:

> The Christian faithful are those who, inasmuch as they have been incorporated in Christ through baptism, have been constituted as the people of God; for this reason, since they have become sharers in Christ's priestly, prophetic and royal office in their own manner, they are called to exercise the mission which God has entrusted to the Church to fulfill in the world, in accord with the condition proper to each one.
>
> This Church, constituted and organized as a society in this world, subsists in the Catholic Church, governed by the successor of Peter and the bishops in communion with him.[13]

The council did not further define the interpretation of "subsists." For example, it did not say that the church of Christ subsists "only" in the Catholic Church. Interestingly, Pope John Paul II expanded the concept by saying that among Catholics, the universal church subsists in the particular (diocesan) churches:

> The Catholic Church herself subsists in each particular church, which can be truly complete only through effective communion in faith, sacraments and unity with the whole body of Christ. Last November, in my letter to you during your meeting in Washington . . . I wrote: . . . It is precisely because you are pastors of particular churches in which subsists the fullness of the universal church that you are, and must always be, in full communion with the successor of Peter.[14]

The Catechism of the Catholic Church controlled any expanded interpretation of "subsists." It accepted the basic principle that baptism establishes a bond of unity, but it distinguished among the baptized those "not yet in full communion" with the Catholic Church. The

---

[13] CCL, canons 204/1 and 2.

[14] John Paul II, Address to U.S. Bishops, 12 September 1987, *Origins* 17/16 (1 October 1987) 258.

expression "not yet" revealed the Catholic belief that everyone else's baptism tends toward Catholic communion:

> Baptism constitutes the foundation of communion among all Christians, including those who are not yet in full communion with the Catholic Church: "For men who believe in Christ and have been properly baptized are put in some, though imperfect, communion with the Catholic Church. Justified by faith in Baptism, [they] are incorporated into Christ; they therefore have a right to be called Christians, and with good reason are accepted as brothers by the children of the Catholic Church." "Baptism therefore constitutes *the sacramental bond of unity* existing among all who through it are reborn."[15]

Other words have been more conciliatory. Pope John Paul II wrote about the importance of ecumenism in his encyclical, *Ut unum sint*. He echoed a theme from the World Council of Churches—unity is the will of Christ, and baptism compels believers toward it. The title of the encyclical comes from John 17:22, where Jesus prays at the Last Supper for the unity of his disciples. John Paul says this prayer becomes the duty of the Body of Christ,

> On the eve of his sacrifice on the Cross, Jesus himself prayed to the Father for his disciples and for all those who believe in him, that they *might be one*, a living communion. This is the basis not only of the duty, but also of the responsibility before God and his plan, which falls to those who through Baptism become members of the Body of Christ, a Body in which the fullness of reconciliation and communion must be made present. How is it possible to remain divided, if we have been "buried" through Baptism in the Lord's death, in the very act by which God, through the death of his Son, has broken down the walls of division? Division "openly contradicts the will of Christ, provides a stumbling block to the world, and inflicts damage on the most holy cause of proclaiming the Good News to every creature."[16]

Even more significantly, John Paul acknowledged the strength of the communion that exists among all the baptized. He stated that to some

---

[15] *Catechism of the Catholic Church* 1271, citing *Unitatis redintegratio* 3 and 22/2.
[16] John Paul II, *Ut unum sint* 6, AAS 77 (1995) 925, citing *Unitatis redintegratio*, 1 (See ch. 3 n. 60).

extent, "the one Church of Christ is effectively present" in other Christian Communities. This expression sounds not far from the word "subsists," which is used to describe how the church of Christ resides in the Catholic Church. John Paul's terminology for these bodies is noteworthy too: not heretics, not churches, not ecclesial communities, but "other Christian Communities":

> Indeed, the elements of sanctification and truth present in the other Christian Communities, in a degree which varies from one to the other, constitute the objective basis of the communion, albeit imperfect, which exists between them and the Catholic Church.
>   To the extent that these elements are found in other Christian Communities, the one Church of Christ is effectively present in them. For this reason the Second Vatican Council speaks of a certain, though imperfect communion. The Dogmatic Constitution *Lumen gentium* stresses that the Catholic Church "recognizes that in many ways she is linked" with these Communities by a true union in the Holy Spirit.[17]

However, in speaking of the church's ecumenical commitment, the pope referred not to dialogue but, rather, the imperatives of evangelization:

> Together with all Christ's disciples, the Catholic Church bases upon God's plan her ecumenical commitment to gather all Christians into unity. Indeed, "the Church is not a reality closed in on herself. Rather, she is permanently open to missionary and ecumenical endeavor, for she is sent to the world to announce and witness, to make present and spread the mystery of communion which is essential to her, and to gather all people and all things into Christ, so as to be for all an 'inseparable sacrament of unity.'"[18]

Still, dialogues have continued. Catholics and Lutherans passed a milestone in their 1999 Joint Declaration on the Doctrine of Justification by Faith. That declaration states that through baptism the Holy Spirit lays a foundation for the whole Christian life:

[17] Ibid., 11, AAS 77:927–28, citing *Lumen gentium* 15.
[18] Ibid., 5, AAS 77:924, citing Congregation for the Doctrine of the Faith, Letter to the Bishops of the Catholic Church on Some Aspects of the Church Understood as Communion, *Communionis notio* (28 May 1992) 4; AAS 85 (1993) 840.

We confess together that sinners are justified by faith in the saving action of God in Christ. By the action of the Holy Spirit in baptism, they are granted the gift of salvation, which lays the basis for the whole Christian life. They place their trust in God's gracious promise by justifying faith, which includes hope in God and love for him. Such a faith is active in love and thus the Christian cannot and should not remain without works. But whatever in the justified precedes or follows the free gift of faith is neither the basis of justification nor merits it.[19]

These postconciliar declarations and others helped deepen Christians' understanding of the bond of unity that exists among all the baptized, as well as its implications for evangelization and salvation. At the same time, they revealed the caution with which the Catholic Church expresses its ecclesiology.

DOMINUS IESUS

More controversial, however, was a Declaration of the Congregation for the Doctrine of the Faith called *Dominus Iesus*, promulgated in 2000.

The timing proved ironic. Pope John Paul II had announced the Jubilee Year as a time that would bring rejoicing to the world, as it recalled the anniversary of the birth of the Savior:

The term *jubilee* speaks of joy; not just an inner joy but a jubilation which is manifested outwardly, for the coming of God is also an outward, visible, audible and tangible event, as St. John makes clear (cf. 1 Jn 1:1). It is thus appropriate that every sign of joy at this coming should have its own outward expression. This will demonstrate that the church rejoices in salvation. She invites everyone to rejoice, and she tries to create conditions to ensure that the power of salvation may be shared by all. Hence the year 2000 will be celebrated as the Great Jubilee.[20]

But during that year, certain comments by the Congregation for the Doctrine of the Faith were not joyfully received by many Christians. In *Dominius Iesus* the Congregation states that the church of Christ exists "fully only in the Catholic Church":

[19] Lutheran World Federation and the Catholic Church, *Joint Declaration on the Doctrine of Justification* (1999) 25.
[20] John Paul II, *Tertio millennio adveniente* 16, AAS 77 (1995) 15.

The Catholic faithful *are required to profess* that there is an historical continuity—rooted in the apostolic succession—between the Church founded by Christ and the Catholic Church: "This is the single Church of Christ . . . which our Saviour, after his resurrection, entrusted to Peter's pastoral care (cf. Jn 21:17), commissioning him and the other Apostles to extend and rule her (cf. Mt 28:18ff.), erected for all ages as 'the pillar and mainstay of the truth' (1 Tim 3:15). This Church, constituted and organized as a society in the present world, subsists in [*subsistit in*] the Catholic Church, governed by the Successor of Peter and by the Bishops in communion with him." With the expression *subsistit in*, the Second Vatican Council sought to harmonize two doctrinal statements: on the one hand, that the Church of Christ, despite the divisions which exist among Christians, continues to exist fully only in the Catholic Church, and on the other hand, that "outside of her structure, many elements can be found of sanctification and truth," that is, in those Churches and ecclesial communities which are not yet in full communion with the Catholic Church. But with respect to these, it needs to be stated that "they derive their efficacy from the very fullness of grace and truth entrusted to the Catholic Church."[21]

Furthermore, the Congregation explained the distinction between churches and ecclesial communities. The Second Vatican Council had used these terms,[22] but did not otherwise define them. George H. Tavard, who attended the Council as a peritus, says,

The one and only reason why the formula "Churches and Ecclesial Communities of the West" was used in the decree on ecumenism was that the Salvation Army and the Society of Friends were represented by official observers, and that they do not regard themselves as churches. We nevertheless wanted to indicate that there is something ecclesial about them. In fact when the archbishop of Westminster, John Carmel Heenan, introduced that

---

[21] Congregation for the Doctrine of the Faith, "Declaration '*Dominus Iesus*': On the Unicity and Salvific Universality of Jesus Christ and the Church," 16, citing the Second Vatican Council and various fathers of the church. *Origins* 30/14 (September 14, 2000) 216.

[22] E.g., *Lumen gentium* 15 and *Unitatis redintegratio* 4. They also appear in RCIA 473. National Statutes 30 and 33 (see RCIA Appendix III), and CCL 874/2.

section of the decree to the council, before discussion and vote, he explicitly said: "It is not our intention to decide what is a church and what is not a church."[23]

Nevertheless, in *Dominus Iesus* the Congregation wrote,

> [T]he ecclesial communities which have not preserved the valid Episcopate and the genuine and integral substance of the Eucharistic mystery, are not Churches in the proper sense; however, those who are baptized in these communities are, by Baptism, incorporated in Christ and thus are in a certain communion, albeit imperfect, with the Church. Baptism in fact tends *per se* toward the full development of life in Christ, through the integral profession of faith, the Eucharist, and full communion in the Church.[24]

Whereas many other Christians believe every valid baptism leads to church membership, which leads to communion, the Congregation stated that some valid baptisms incorporate one into Christ but into an imperfect communion with the church. The Congregation also stated that "church" is not an appropriate term for many Christian bodies.[25]

Furthermore, a footnote in *Dominus Iesus* cautions against a broader interpretation of "subsists":

> The interpretation of those who would derive from the formula *subsistit in* the thesis that the one Church of Christ could subsist also in non-Catholic Churches and ecclesial communities is therefore contrary to the authentic meaning of *Lumen gentium*. "The Council instead chose the word *subsistit* precisely to clarify that there exists only one 'subsistence' of the true Church, while outside her visible structure there only exist *elementa Ecclesiae*, which—being elements of that same Church—tend and lead toward the Catholic Church."[26]

---

[23] George H. Tavard, 21 February 2006 email to author. See also the *relatio* on the third chapter of the decree on ecumenism offered by Archbishop John Heenan of Westminster in *Acta synodalia* 3:5, 13–15.

[24] *Dominus Iesus*, 17.

[25] Ironically, there are many "churches" that think that Catholics are not "Christians."

[26] Footnote 56, citing Congregation for the Doctrine of the Faith, Notification on the Book *Church: Charism and Power* by Father Leonardo Boff: AAS 77 (1985) 758–59.

These precisions provoked strong reactions. The Congregation seemed deaf to the reality that many groups call themselves "churches," many have bonded as a "World Council of Churches," and that the word is used colloquially in a much broader sense. Adrian Hastings argued that the Anglican Communion is indeed a church:

> Could it really be thought plausible that Pope John Paul II was not in a real way treating the Anglican Communion as a sister Church when he sat and knelt beside Archbishop Runcie in Canterbury Cathedral, or when he invited Archbishop Carey to join him and a representative of the Patriarch of Constantinople in opening the Holy Door at the start of this jubilee year? Examples of such implicit recognition could be multiplied. If the Pope gave Henry Chadwick a stole, the special symbol of the priesthood, was it in order for Professor Chadwick to celebrate an invalid Eucharist?[27]

Hastings adds that Pope Paul VI called the Anglican Communion an "ever-beloved sister."

Archbishop Rembert Weakland of Milwaukee wrote about his perceptions of the document's deficiencies:

> What is disappointing about this document is that so many of our partners in ecumenical dialogues will find its tone heavy, almost arrogant and condescending. To them it is bound to seem out of keeping with the elevated and open tone of the documents of Vatican Council II. It ignores all of the ecumenical dialogues of the last 35 years, as if they did not exist. None of the agreed statements are cited. Has no progress in working toward convergence of theological thought occurred in 35 years?[28]

Francis A. Sullivan believed that the Congregation did not restate the council's use of the term "subsists in," but redefined it:

> [It] is helpful to recall that the official Catholic doctrine prior to the council—as expressed, for instance in the encyclical *Mystici Corporis* of Pius XII—was that the church of Christ is strictly and exclusively identified with the Catholic Church. . . . The intention

[27] Adrian Hastings, "Sisters for All That," *The Tablet*, 21 October 2000, 1411.
[28] Rembert Weakland, "On the Document's Ecumenical Impact," *Origins* 30/17 (October 5, 2000) 267.

[of Vatican II] clearly was to continue to make a positive statement about the Catholic Church, but without the negative implication that the previous doctrine of exclusive identity had regarding the other churches. However, the Theological Commission did not spell out in detail how the term "subsists in" was to be understood.[29]

Sullivan says that the Congregation has reinterpreted the term "subsists" to mean "continues to exist fully."

Richard McBrien, in a talk given at the Centro Pro Unione in Rome, further clarified the matter:

> . . . *Dominus Iesus* does *not* say that the Church of Christ continues to exist "only" in the Catholic Church; it says that it is only in the Catholic Church that it continues to exist "*fully*" (n. 16, my emphasis). . . .
>
> Indeed, it was the teaching of Pius XII, in his encyclicals *Mystici corporis* and *Humani generis*, that the Catholic Church and the Mystical Body of Christ are "one and the same" ("*unum idemque esse*"). . . .
>
> . . . In changing the verb from "*est*" to "*subsistit in*" the council fathers clearly intended to include non-Catholic churches and ecclesial communities in the one, albeit divided, Body of Christ.[30]

In the end, nevertheless, *Dominus Iesus* sheds light on what is meant by the title of the rite Catholics use to receive into membership those who are validly baptized: The Rite of Reception of Baptized Christians into the Full Communion of the Catholic Church. It is not communion "with" the Catholic Church, as if someone *outside* the church might have communion *with* the church. There is one full communion, and the baptized Christian is being received into it in the Catholic Church. The church believes that one's baptism is already tending toward communion, but communion is not full until after reception.

Many have taken offense that *Dominus Iesus* refused to use the term "churches" to define the ecclesial bodies formed after the Reformation. But in an irenic interpretation, *Dominus Iesus* says they are not

[29] Francis A. Sullivan, "The Impact of *Dominus Iesus* on Ecumenism," *America* 183/11 (October 28, 2000) 8–9.

[30] Richard McBrien, "*Dominus Iesus*: An Ecclesiological Critique," *Centro Pro Unione Semi-Annual Bulletin* 59 (Spring 2001) 19–20.

"churches" in the fullest sense because they are already part of the one holy apostolic "Church." It would be divisive for all Christians to call the various bodies "churches." But, of course, the word is used colloquially in a different sense. To call one's neighbors members of the Lutheran Church is handier than saying they are part of the Lutheran Ecclesial Community, a moniker that Lutherans would not recognize anyway. Besides, etymologically, "ecclesial community" sounds like a circumlocution for "church." But the main point, stated less stridently, might have won more collective agreement—that there is one church, and all Christians belong to it.

Some Catholics like to say that the Catholic Church is the "one true church" and that people join it because they are coming to the truth. But neither the Second Vatican Council nor the Congregation for the Doctrine of the Faith choose those words. *Lumen gentium* backed away from them, *Dominus Iesus* came closer to them, but neither has adopted the old formula. The one true church is the church of Jesus Christ, and it subsists in the Catholic Church.

The Congregation stated that the church of Christ continues to exist fully only in the Catholic Church. But many Christian theologians can accept this only if the term "Catholic Church" is used in the broadest sense of the one, holy, catholic church of the baptized faithful who profess a common creed. Common baptism should tend toward communion.

The Second Vatican Council certainly meant to chart new waters with the expression "subsists in." It abandoned the verb "is" in favor of one that sounded more sensitive. Even the neologism "ecclesial community" goes a step further than calling other bodies "heretics." The ecumenical movement has come a long way, but it has a long way to go as precisions in language and theological meaning come to light.

Christians switching from one church to another are seeking a community where their faith will be better nourished and supported. Their journey toward spiritual fullness is a microcosm of the great ecclesial journey toward fullness of union and fullness of life.

ECUMENICAL STATEMENTS

While weathering the storm of *Dominus Iesus*, the ecumenical dialogue has continued. Partners in dialogue are serious about expressing more solidarity about the implications of a common baptism. For example, in 2002, ecumenical partners in Germany agreed on the same theology of baptism and on the same valid administration of the rite.

Based on the unity in baptism given in Christ and the common aim to avoid all misunderstandings concerning the valid administration of baptism, the joint declaration affirms the communion between all baptized which is grounded in their communion with the triune God through baptism, the orientation to a common expression of faith and to a eucharistic communion through baptism and the call to overcome all divisions among the churches.[31]

Older agreements should not be forgotten. The Australian Episcopal Conference and the Uniting Church in Australia said,

All Christians are baptized into the one Christ and share in the life of the Holy Trinity; their Baptism is entry into the one Church of Christ which is the great sign of the unity of mankind. One in Christ, the community is sent into the world to bear witness to Christ's redeeming work. The one Baptism which Christians share looks forward to its fulfillment in the one visible Church in which all will share the one faith, the same ministry and the same sacraments.[32]

In Belgium five dialogue partners released this statement: "Baptism already creates a real link, that attaches all the baptized in Christ and unites them with each other; in faith, hope and charity."[33]

Other groups have spoken out similarly in nations such as France, Poland, Taiwan, and the Philippines.[34] The hope for "eucharistic hospitality" remains alive in the Pontifical Council for Promoting Christian Unity and among its dialogue partners:

The central question behind the discussions leading to mutual recognition has to do with ecclesiology. The agreements on mutual

[31] "Study Documents for This Plenary," *Information Service: Pontifical Council for Promoting Christian Unity* 109 (2002/I–II), 23, citing *Vereinbarung zwischen der Evangelischen Kirche im Rheinland und dem Erzbistum Köln sowie den Bistümern Aachen, Essen, Münster und Trier zur gegenseitigen Anerkennung der Taufe.* See also *Die Sakraamente (Mysterien) der Engliederung in die Kirche.*

[32] Ibid., 23–24, citing "A Common Understanding of Baptism," Joint Statement by the Roman Catholic Church and the Uniting Church in Australia, 1979.

[33] Ibid., 24, citing "Declaration de reconnaissance interecclesiale du baptême," Bruxelles, 1971.

[34] Ibid.

recognition of baptism reflect the present stage of a changed ecumenical situation. . . . This is all the more urgent given the
prevalent idea among some dialogue partners that common baptism is sufficient for a certain form of communion that could be
expressed in eucharistic hospitality in the Catholic Church.[35]

Catholics excited to receive individual Christians into communion
also hunger for real ecclesial unity among all Christians, East and
West. When a parish receives an individual into the full communion
of the Catholic Church, it should not lose the vision of ecumenical
dialogue. Christians fundamentally experience one baptism, but not
so much one church and one communion. If ecumenical dialogue can
close the gaps between Christian bodies, it will diminish the need to
celebrate a rite of reception for individual Christians.

---

[35] Ibid., 24–25.

Part IV

In Search of Communion

Chapter 8

Discerning Readiness

The historical and theological foundations discussed in Parts II and III lie behind the rite of reception that now rests in the hands of Catholic parish ministers. These ministers make some choices regarding the implementation of this rite. And the choices affect the apprehension of an authentic theology of baptism on behalf of those in search of communion.

CATECHIZED AND UNCATECHIZED

Other Christians are deemed ready to become Catholic when they express a desire to do so and when parish leaders are satisfied that they have a sufficient understanding of the step they are taking. They are also expected to confess their sins before they are received. In many parishes, another factor determines their reception: the date of Easter. Many parishes receive baptized Christians into the church at the Easter Vigil to simplify the demands on catechists by having them prepare baptized candidates together with catechumens and to give candidates the celebratory framework of the Vigil for their reception.

The Rite of Christian Initiation of Adults offers only a little help in determining readiness. The book is a ritual text, not a catechetical one. The original text made no statement about how to structure the formation of candidates for reception. In the case of baptized, uncatechized *Catholics*, the original text envisioned a process similar to the catechumenate. "For the most part the plan of catechesis corresponds to the one laid down for catechumens."[1] The American edition of the rite added to this group baptized, uncatechized Christians of other faiths.[2]

---

[1] RCIA 402.
[2] RCIA 400.

However, some of those joining from other Christian bodies may have already had good formation and experience. For this reason the National Statutes in the United States distinguish those who have "relatively little Christian upbringing" from "those who have lived as Christians":

> Those who have been baptized but have received relatively little Christian upbringing may participate in the elements of catechumenal formation so far as necessary and appropriate, but should not take part in rites intended for the unbaptized catechumens. . . . Those baptized persons who have lived as Christians and need only instruction in the Catholic tradition and a degree of probation within the Catholic community should not be asked to undergo a full program parallel to the catechumenate.[3]

This distinction recognizes the validity of the baptism already received as well as the Christian life already lived. Those who have been following Christ need not undergo the entire formation expected of those who have not. The formation is to be adapted to the needs of the individual:

> The baptized Christian is to receive both doctrinal and spiritual preparation, adapted to individual pastoral requirements, for reception into the full communion of the Catholic Church. The candidate should learn to deepen an inner adherence to the Church, where he or she will find the fullness of his or her baptism.[4]

The National Statutes reecho this point:

> Those who have already been baptized in another Church or ecclesial community should not be treated as catechumens or so designated. Their doctrinal and spiritual preparation for reception into full Catholic communion should be determined according to the individual case, that is, it should depend on the extent to which the baptized person has led a Christian life within a community of faith and been appropriately catechized to deepen his or her inner adherence to the Church.[5]

---

[3] National Statutes 31 (see RCIA Appendix III).
[4] RCIA 477.
[5] National Statutes 30.

The rite envisions that the ceremony will not place unnecessary burdens on those who wish to be received. Logically, the preparation should share this restraint:

> The rite is so arranged that no greater burden than necessary (see Acts 15:28) is required for the establishment of communion and unity.[6]

Eastern Orthodox Christians who enter the fullness of Catholic communion should have a limited formation. The Catholic Church recognizes the validity of their sacraments, so it needs only to verify the desire of individuals and to ensure their basic understanding of the step they are taking.[7]

Underlying the discernment of readiness is the question of sufficient catechesis: When is a person considered "catechized"? One answer is "Never." Every Christian continues to be formed in the faith throughout life. Some level of catechesis should be attained before a baptized Christian becomes a Catholic, but there is no single list of doctrines to be learned or beliefs to be professed apart from the Creed.

The object of catechesis is Jesus Christ. All the baptized should already know Christ. Our catechesis deepens our appreciation of him. John Paul II expressed this eloquently:

> At the heart of catechesis, we find, in essence, a Person, the Person of Jesus of Nazareth. . . . Catechizing is in a way to lead a person to study this Mystery in all its dimensions. . . . It is therefore to reveal in the Person of Christ the whole of God's eternal design reaching fulfillment in that Person. . . . The definitive aim of catechesis is to put people not only in touch but in communion, in intimacy, with Jesus Christ.[8]

The General Directory for Catechesis says initiatory catechesis is a

> Comprehensive formation [that] includes more than instruction: it is an apprenticeship of the entire Christian life, it is a "complete Christian initiation" [Catechesi tradendi 21], which promotes an

---

[6] RCIA 473.

[7] However, the Catholic Church is not to proselytize those in Orthodoxy. Cf. the Code of Oriental Law, canon 31. Such an action among Catholics would provoke a penalty in the Code of Canon Law, 1465.

[8] John Paul II, Catechesi tradendi 5, AAS 71 (1979) 1280–81.

authentic following of Christ, focused on his Person; it implies education in knowledge of the faith and in the life of faith, in such a manner that the entire person, at his deepest levels, feels enriched by the word of God.[9]

Mary Birmingham outlines the six tasks of catechesis appearing in paragraphs 85 and 86 of the *General Directory for Catechesis*:

> Initiation catechesis is a proclamation . . . of Jesus Christ (knowledge of the faith). It is an invitation to pray as Jesus prayed (teaching to pray). . . . [It] is to promote an understanding of the liturgy and sacraments (liturgical education). . . . It forms disciples to live a life in Christian community . . . (education for communal life). Catechesis promotes moral transformation . . . (moral formation). Catechesis forms people in a life of prayer, in praise of God and for apostolic service, mission and witness (missionary initiation).[10]

These directives help determine what catechesis is sufficient, while they give pastoral leaders the flexibility to discern readiness individually with the persons in question.

James Dunning proposed a fourfold analysis of the candidate's spiritual journey, based on the elements that make up catechetical formation for the unbaptized in the period of the catechumenate.[11] During that time, "A suitable catechesis is provided." Catechumens "become familiar with the Christian way of life." The church helps them with "suitable liturgical rites." And they "learn how to work actively with others to spread the Gospel." Dunning says every candidate stands somewhere on each of four different continua based on these categories of formation: word, worship, community, and service.[12]

---

[9] Congregation for the Clergy, *General Directory for Catechesis* (Washington: United States Catholic Conference, 1997) 67.

[10] Mary Birmingham, "Catechumenate and Doctrine," in *Institute Resource Packet: Serving the Initiation and Reconciliation Ministries* (Washington DC: North American Forum on the Catechumenate, 2004) 35.

[11] RCIA 75.

[12] Oakham, "Formation of Catechized Christians," in *One at the Table*, 131. He draws this chart from comments by Dunning, who credits John Butler of St. Augustine Parish in Washington, DC. with the basic idea. See Dunning, "What Is a Catechized Adult?" *Forum Newsletter* 9, no. 3 (Summer, 1992) 1, 4, 6.

On the word continuum, people stand somewhere between a "literalist understanding" of the bible and an "understanding of its meaning." For example, someone may move from believing that God created the world in exactly six days to an understanding that the first chapters of Genesis teach more broadly the meaning that God is the Creator. In terms of worship, people stand somewhere in a continuum between "privatistic prayer" and "public worship." Thus they may move from attending Mass because it is a convenient time to pray in silence to engaging in a more full and conscious participation in the communal worship of the church. On the community continuum, people stand somewhere between "rugged individualism" and "communal interdependence." We see this when someone moves from making purchases that improve his or her own status to giving more to the needy. Closely related is the service continuum, where people stand between "concern for one's own salvation" to "witnessing for the salvation of the world." For example, someone may move from performing good deeds in order to be personally saved to performing acts of witness, charity, and justice for the benefit of others.

These continua are helpful for exploring the doctrinal and spiritual values of candidates, but they also work for catechumens. Candidates already bring a Christ-centered experience of faith, worship, and action to these areas, and that should serve as the starting point for analyzing their spiritual needs.

Dunning declares absurd the rite's minimal expectations of catechesis:

> [It] seems to equate uncatechized with those baptized as infants who "did not receive further catechetical formation nor, consequently, the sacraments of confirmation and eucharist" (#400). Put that sentence positively, and a catechized adult apparently is anyone who had catechetical formation as a child and who has celebrated confirmation and eucharist. That seems to equate catechesis of adults with the very beginnings of the formation of children (which may be not catechesis but merely cognitive instruction) and to assume that all who completed initiation in confirmation and eucharist have since then become catechized adults.[13]

---

[13] Dunning, "What Is a Catechized Adult?" 1 (see n. 12).

Nonetheless, readiness can be determined once parish ministers grasp what candidates should be ready for. Candidates should already be following Christ. The question is whether they are ready to be received into the full communion of the Catholic Church. Much of their preparation, then, should be focused on their Catholic identity. [14]

In the ritual, they will profess the creed and state their acceptance of what the Catholic Church teaches. They are ready when they know enough to make that statement with integrity.

CONFESSION

Candidates are also expected to confess their sins before the rite of reception:

> If the profession of faith and reception take place within Mass, the candidate, according to his or her own conscience, should make a confession of sins beforehand, first informing the confessor that he or she is about to be received into full communion. Any confessor who is lawfully approved may hear the candidate's confession. [15]

"Any confessor" may do this. There was a time in church history when people had to confess to their own pastor. And there had been more recent opinions that the priest who received the candidate had to be the one who heard his or her confession. But the church was anxious to separate the confession of sins from the act of reception, so no one would think that reception constituted reconciliation from the sin of heresy. The National Statutes concur:

---

[14] In catechumenate formation, this point is often missed. Some parishes prepare catechumens as if they are converting to the Catholic Church, not to Christ. But the primary conversion for those who are unbaptized is always conversion to Jesus Christ. See Turner, "Catholic Initiation or Christian Initiation of Adults?" *Catechumenate: A Journal of Christian Initiation* 26/1 (January 2004) 21–33.

[15] RCIA 482. If the candidate is a baptized but uncatechized Catholic adult seeking First Communion, "penitential services should be arranged in such a way as to prepare these adults for the celebration of the sacrament of penance" (RCIA 408). The National Statutes say, "The celebration of the sacrament of reconciliation with [Catholic] candidates for confirmation and eucharist is to be carried out at a time prior to and distinct from the celebration of confirmation and the eucharist" (27).

> The celebration of the sacrament of reconciliation with candidates for reception into full communion is to be carried out at a time prior to and distinct from the celebration of the rite of reception.[16]

These statements lay out the expectation that baptized candidates will confess their sins before they are received. Still, the expectation is not absolute. The first statement limits the expectation to the circumstance when reception is celebrated "within Mass." But this alludes to First Communion; candidates should confess their sins before receiving communion for the first time at the Mass of their reception. Although the document does not state so, it would surely expect the person received into the church outside of Mass to go to confession before receiving communion.

Even so, the document says the candidates "should" make a confession—not "must" make one. Only those in mortal sin are required by law to confess their sins before receiving communion.[17] To require confession of every candidate would imply that each one is in mortal sin. From a historical perspective, that would suggest that the preconciliar rites for other Christians becoming Catholic—abjuration from heresy and absolution—were simply displaced with the postconciliar rites in which the candidate confesses before the rite of reception, not during it.

Still, one should not lightly dismiss a candidate from the sacrament of reconciliation. Candidates should make a confession. They deserve the opportunity to experience the sacramental mercy of God.

Joseph Favazza says reconciliation is integral to initiation. "[R]econciliation, like initiation, is conversion into, commitment to, and celebration in, community." He promotes the reconciliation of candidates not because they have lived in heretical sin but because they are making a commitment to a new community.[18] Indeed, sacramental reconciliation can be a life-changing experience for Christians, an opportunity to admit aloud sorrow for one's sins and to hear the

[16] National Statutes 36.

[17] Canon 916 obliges those conscious of grave sin not to share communion without previous sacramental confession. Canon 988/2 says confession is "recommended" for the faithful guilty of venial sins. See Turner, "First Confession Before First Communion: Settled or Unsettling?" *Liturgical Catechesis* 5/3 (June–July 2002) 8–9.

[18] "Reconciliation as Second Baptism," Joseph A. Favazza, in *One at the Table*, 48.

church's minister extend the mercy of Christ. It can be a moment of powerful healing for those who have made this spiritual journey deeply—not just as a shift from one faith community to another but as a recommitment to Jesus Christ and his church.

The ecumenical directory permits other Christians to celebrate the sacrament of penance under certain circumstances:

> Catholic ministers may lawfully administer the sacraments of penance, Eucharist and the anointing of the sick to members of the Eastern Churches, who ask for these sacraments of their own free will and are properly disposed. In these particular cases also, due consideration should be given to the discipline of the Eastern Churches for their own faithful and any suggestion of proselytism should be avoided.[19]

> The conditions under which a Catholic minister may administer the sacraments of the Eucharist, of penance and of the anointing of the sick to a baptized person . . . are that the person be unable to have recourse for the sacrament desired to a minister of his or her own Church or ecclesial Community, ask for the sacrament of his or her own initiative, manifest Catholic faith in this sacrament and be properly disposed.[20]

Parish leaders discern the readiness of baptized candidates who come to them for reception. They make their judgment based on the validity of baptism, the candidates' understanding of the Catholic Church, their openness to the sacrament of reconciliation, and their desire to be received. The candidates discern readiness in a similar way. If their intellect grasps what they are doing, and if their will desires it, they are probably ready. When the candidate and the parish leadership agree, the rite of reception may be celebrated. They need not wait until Easter.

DIVORCED AND REMARRIED CANDIDATES

If baptized Christians wishing to become Catholic are divorced and remarried, or if they are married to someone in that situation, an annulment on the previous marriage(s) must be obtained from the

---

[19] Pontifical Council for Promoting Christian Unity, *Directory for the Application of Principles and Norms on Ecumenism* 125, citing CCL 844/3.
[20] Ibid., 131.

Catholic Church, and the current marriage must be convalidated in the presence of a deacon or priest. Even if a previous marriage did not take place in a church ceremony, the Catholic Church considers the first marriage valid. It amazes many people that the Catholic Church legislates the validity of the marriage of people who are not Catholic. But the church presumes the validity of every first marriage. If a couple says "till death do us part," the church takes them at their word. Before a divorced person can be married in a Catholic ceremony, the validity of any previous marriage must be investigated.

The rite of reception is delayed until these matters are resolved because the meaning of the ceremony involves communion. A divorced, remarried person (or someone married to such a person) is eligible for communion in the Catholic Church only after annulment and convalidation. Without those steps a priest is not free to receive a previously baptized Christian into the church. Stories are told of priests who receive a divorced and remarried person into the church while deferring communion. However, the integrity of the rite of reception needs to be maintained. There is no point in receiving someone into the "full communion" of the Catholic Church if the reception does not include the right to communion.

If a baptized candidate is divorced and single, an annulment is not required for the rite of reception. Even divorced Catholics retain access to the Eucharist unless they marry again outside the church without having previously obtained an annulment.

Again, Easter is not the only time of year when candidates may be received. If annulments need more time than expected, the rite of reception may be celebrated whenever the candidate is ready.

Chapter 9

Ritual Issues

THE MASS "FOR THE UNITY OF CHRISTIANS"

When the rite of reception is celebrated apart from a Sunday or a solemnity, the Mass "For the Unity of Christians" from the Masses for Various Needs and Occasions may be used. The Sacramentary offers a choice for the opening prayer, prayer over the gifts, preface, and communion prayer. The Lectionary proposes a selection of Scriptures.

Sundays and solemnities are ideal occasions for celebration because the local community will be gathered for worship. Still, the texts for this Mass merit examination. The Mass texts take a broad ecumenical view, while the ritual guides the reception of one Christian into the Catholic Church. The ceremony tests the proposition from the Decree on Ecumenism "that the work of preparation and reconciliation of those individuals who desire full Catholic communion is different in nature from an ecumenical undertaking. But there is no opposition because both proceed from the marvelous direction of God."[1]

The Sacramentary texts look to a day when Christians will be united in baptism, church, and communion. There are six options for the opening prayer, the first of which doubles as one of the general intercessions on Good Friday. It says, "We are all consecrated to you by our common baptism; make us one in the fullness of faith and keep us one in the fellowship of love." The second prays, "May we live in a manner worthy of our calling; make us witnesses of your truth to all men and help us work to bring all believers together in the unity of faith and the fellowship of peace." Another bids, "Make us able and willing to do what you ask. May the people you call to your kingdom be one in

---

[1] *Unitatis redintegratio* 4, AAS 57:95.

faith and love." Yet another: "Lord, hear the prayers of your people and bring the hearts of believers together in your praise and in common sorrow for their sins. Heal all divisions among Christians that we may rejoice in the perfect unity of your Church and move together as one to eternal life in your kingdom." The last two prayers ask for the gift and power of the Spirit over God's people. "May they study and work together for perfect unity among Christians"; and "Remove divisions among Christians. Let your Church rise more clearly as a sign for all the nations that the world may be filled with the light of your Spirit and believe in Jesus Christ whom you have sent." The prayers over the gifts and after communion make similar petitions for unity, peace, charity, and love.[2]

The preface for the Mass for Christian unity praises God for the diversity of the gifts of the Spirit. It presumes that unity already exists: "Through Christ you bring us to the knowledge of your truth, that we may be united by one faith and one baptism to become his body. Through Christ you have given the Holy Spirit to all peoples. How wonderful are the works of the Spirit, revealed in so many gifts! Yet how marvelous is the unity the Spirit creates from their diversity, as he dwells in the hearts of your children, filling the whole Church with his presence and guiding it with his wisdom!"[3]

The Sacramentary texts offer a fairly unified vision of Christian Unity, but the Lectionary texts are more complex. From the Old Testament the Lectionary recommends a choice of these: Moses tells the people that God will gather them from all the nations where he scattered them (Deuteronomy 30:1-4). Ezekiel prophesies that God will take the people away from the Gentile nations, gather them from all the foreign lands, and bring them back to their own land (36:24-28). The same prophet takes two sticks, representing Judah and Joseph, and joins them together as a sign of unity: God will take the children of Israel from among the nations and bring them back to their land (Ezekiel 37:15-19, 21b-22, 26-28). Zephaniah prophesies that God will bring the children of Zion home and gather them (3:16b-20). All these passages see the restoration of exiled and scattered Israel as a foreshadowing of the restoration of a divided Christianity. The image is rich, but put in the

[2] For Unity of Christians, 13 A, B, and C from *Masses and Prayers for Various Needs and Occasions* (New York: Catholic Book Publishing Co., 1985).

[3] Ibid., 76.

context of the rite of reception, this ritual appears to be an example of how the restoration will happen: Protestants will become Catholic, one by one.

Among the epistle options, Paul tells the Corinthians that their divisions are intolerable (1 Cor 1:10-13). The Letter to the Ephesians, apparently to a Gentile audience, announces that the readers are strangers and sojourners no longer; rather, they are members of God's household, the dwelling place of the Spirit (2:19-22). The same letter makes an appeal to preserve the unity of the Spirit, for there is one Lord, one faith and one baptism (Eph 4:1-6). Ephesians also asks that those who were sealed by the Holy Spirit avoid all bitterness and malice and be kind, compassionate, and forgiving (4:30–5:2). Paul asks the Philippians to complete his joy by being of the same mind, with the same love, united in heart, and possessing the attitude of Christ Jesus: humility (2:1-13). The Colossians are asked to let the peace of Christ rule their hearts, the peace into which they were called in one body (3:9b-17). Timothy is told that Jesus is the one mediator between God and humanity (1 Tim 2:5-8). The author of 1 John admonishes his readers to love God as he has loved them; God remains in those who acknowledge that Jesus is his son (4:9-15).

These passages share a vision that Christians should get along. Divisions are present, but they are not so strong that baptism is questioned or the Lord's Supper is not shared. Rather, they admit disagreements and call people back to the original vision of unity and love. Put in the context of the rite of reception, these passages appeal to Christians for greater understanding, even as the local church performs a ritual made necessary because serious divisions remain.

The responsorial psalm options open with a canticle of Jeremiah, "Lord, gather your scattered people" (31:10, 11-12ab, 13-14). The popular refrain for Psalm 23, "The Lord is my shepherd; there is nothing I shall want," acknowledges the common belief of Christians in a God who guides them toward verdant pastures of rest (1-3, 4, 5, 6). Similarly, Psalm 100 prays, "We are his people; the sheep of his flock" (1b-2, 3, 4, 5). The refrain for Psalm 118 functions as a prophecy of the centrality of Jesus Christ: "The stone rejected by the builders has become the cornerstone" (22-23, 25-26, 28). Psalm 122 invites believers to go to the house of the Lord with rejoicing (1-2, 4-5, 6-7, 8-9).

All these psalms celebrate a common vision among believers: There is one God and shepherd, one flock on pilgrimage to one eternal home, for eternal life with Jesus, the cornerstone. Like the preface of the Mass, these texts presume an existing unity. As responsories for the rite of reception, they shimmer with affirmation and hope.

Two of the suggested alleluia verses quote recommended New Testament readings (Eph 4:5-6a and Col 3:15). Another cites Jesus' poignant words, "May they all be one" (John 17:21). Still another says, "Lord, let your Church be gathered from the ends of the earth into your kingdom, for the glory and power are yours through Jesus Christ forever." The image of "gathering" also appeared in the first readings. On one hand, this verse implies that unity will not come until the end of time; on the other, it echoes the Protestant ending to the Lord's Prayer, extending a small olive branch toward ecumenical efforts. The final suggestion for the alleluia verse borrows the imagery of the paschal candle from the Easter Proclamation (Exsultet): "The Church of the Lord is a single light; it shines everywhere, yet the Church is not divided." These texts balance the desire for deeper unity with an affirmation that some unity already exists. The last is especially suited for a meaningful rite of reception.

Among the gospel selections, Jesus tells the disciples that he is there when they gather for prayer, and he encourages them to practice forgiveness (Matt 18:19-22). The disciples see divisions: they want to prevent someone outside their number from casting out demons in Jesus' name and to call down fire from heaven to consume an inhospitable Samaritan village; Jesus will have none of this (Luke 9:49-56). Jesus, the Good Shepherd, says there is one flock (John 10:11-16). Caiaphas unwittingly prophesies that Jesus' death will gather into one all the dispersed children of God (John 11:45-52). Jesus washes the feet of his disciples as an example to them (John 13:1-15). Jesus prays for his disciples, who have kept the Father's word (John 17:1-11a). He also prays that they may be one (John 17:11b-19; and 20-26).[4]

These gospels offer a mix of themes: the unity of the disciples of Jesus, patience with those outside the fold, and service offered to others. In the rite of reception, readings about the separation of Christians can make it appear that this rite is the only path to union. Other gospels underscore the unity that does exist, while they command Christians to serve one another.

---

[4] All texts can be found in the *Lectionary for Mass*, Second Typical Edition, Volume IV (Washington DC: Confraternity of Christian Doctrine, 2001) under "Masses for Various Needs and Occasions"; section I, For the Holy Church; no. 10, For the Unity of Christians.

The danger in selecting readings from this list is that they can make the reception of a baptized Christian look like "Exhibit A" in the quest for Christian unity. In effect, this is what *Dominus Iesus* has said, but ecumenical dialogue has already been building on the unity shared among Christians, which some of these Scripture texts also affirm.

The choice of texts for the Mass "For the Unity of Christians" indicates two dimensions that need not be opposed, but can be: the dialogue among churches and the helping of individual Christians who wish to become Catholic.

THE RECEPTION OF AN ORTHODOX CHRISTIAN

If someone from an Orthodox Church wishes to become Catholic, the reception should be done as simply as possible. "No liturgical rite is required, but simply a profession of Catholic faith, even if such persons are permitted, in virtue of recourse to the Apostolic See, to transfer to the Latin rite."[5] No profession of faith is required, because the Catholic Church believes it shares sufficient faith with the Oriental churches, although there remain some differences on doctrinal matters including the Holy Spirit and the papacy. The celebrant does not administer confirmation, because the Catholic Church believes that the chrismation given at baptism in the Orthodox churches is a sacrament.[6] Instead, when the celebrant receives someone from an Orthodox Church, he places his right hand on the head of the candidate, while proclaiming the act of reception.[7]

When an Orthodox Christian becomes a Catholic, he or she becomes a member of the parallel Eastern Catholic Church, not a member of the Latin (Roman) Church.[8] For example, if Greek Orthodox persons wish to become Catholic, they are received into the Greek Catholic Rite. Ideally, the ceremony takes place in an Eastern Catholic Church, but it may happen in a Roman Catholic Church. If so, the individuals still become Eastern Catholic, not Roman Catholic. If they wish to become Roman Catholic, they make recourse to the Apostolic See. The process is involved, but it can be done.[9] The Roman Church is not

---

[5] RCIA 474, citing the Vatican II's Decree on Eastern Catholic Churches, *Orientalium Ecclesiarum* 25 and 4.

[6] Code of Oriental Law, 897.

[7] RCIA 492.

[8] Code of Oriental Law, 36.

[9] Ibid., 32, 112.

to encourage such transfers but should, rather, support the beauty, endurance, and essence of the Eastern Rites. Such a transfer is not necessary for communion, because Eastern Catholics and Roman Catholics all share at one another's eucharistic tables.

THE RECEPTION OF CHILDREN

Children who are baptized in other Christian communities may also be received into the Catholic Church. This may happen, for example, when one or both parents are received into the church.

The Catholic Church considers children to be "adults" as far as baptism is concerned when they have reached the age of the use of reason:

> What is prescribed in the canons on the baptism of an adult is applicable to all who are no longer infants but have attained the use of reason.[10]

Priests have the faculty to confirm adults (all those who are no longer infants) whom they baptize as well as those they receive into the church. This faculty is granted by the law itself. It need not be obtained from a bishop. It is implicit when the bishop assigns the priest to pastoral duties:

> The following have the faculty of administering confirmation by the law itself:
>
> . . . 2. with regard to the person in question, the presbyter who by reason of office or mandate of the diocesan bishop baptizes one who is no longer an infant or one already baptized whom he admits into the full communion of the Catholic Church.[11]

In the case of a person baptized Catholic as an infant, the bishop is the ordinary minister of confirmation. A priest confirms such a person only with the explicit permission of the bishop.

The second half of this canon speaks of those already baptized, and it makes no distinction about age. The priest has the faculty to confirm "one already baptized whom he admits into the full communion of the Catholic Church." This is not restricted to adults. If the priest con-

[10] CCL 852/1.
[11] CCL 883/2.

ducts the rite of reception, he has the faculty to confirm. This faculty is not optional. The priest is obliged to use it for the spiritual benefit of the individual:

> A presbyter who has this faculty must use it for those in whose favor the faculty was granted.[12]

Consequently, if the priest is receiving a baptized child into the Catholic Church through the rite of reception, he must confirm the child as well. This should win ready approval from the parties involved because the child will benefit from the gifts of the Spirit at a very early age.

However, some people object if the children are younger than the diocesan age of Catholics eligible for confirmation. Such people fear that the church will not have anything to offer the children when their peers are preparing for confirmation. These are legitimate concerns for the establishment of peace and tranquility in the parish. The liturgical documents seem not to have imagined the possibility that young children would be baptized or received into the church at an age much different from the diocesan age of confirmation.[13]

In the United States, the bishops have said that baptized non-Catholic children of catechetical age "will receive the necessary catechesis for confirmation and the eucharist and will receive these sacraments, insofar as possible, at the same time as their classmates."[14] But that is not consonant with the universal documents. A Christian child is to be confirmed when he or she is received into the Catholic Church, not when Catholic classmates are confirmed, unless the classmates will also be confirmed at the rite of reception. The bishops seem to want to avoid the pastoral problems of priests confirming children at an age younger than those confirmed by the bishop, but the law grants the

---

[12] CCL 885/2.

[13] Turner, "Envy and the Confirmation of Children of Catechetical Age," *Catechumenate: A Journal of Christian Initiation* 27/2 (March 2005) 2–10.

[14] NCCB Committee on Liturgy, NCCB Committee on Pastoral Research and Practices, and United States Catholic Conference Committee on Education, "Statement on the Pastoral Challenge of Implementing the Rite of Christian Initiation of Adults for Children Who Have Reached Catechetical Age," March 20, 1990, Bishops' Committee on the Liturgy, *Newsletter* 26 (March 1990) 1.

priest this faculty and commands him to use it.[15] It is for the benefit of the child.

If the baptized child to be received into the Catholic Church is below the age of the use of reason, the rite of reception, confirmation, and communion are not celebrated. Instead, a parent makes a declaration in the presence of the pastor or his delegate. The name of the child is entered into the parish register among those who have been received. Canonist John Huels explains that the juridic act of reception suffices in place of the liturgical act:

> A baptized infant (under seven or lacking the use of reason) may be received into the full communion of the Catholic Church at the request of a Catholic parent or legal guardian. If both parents or the guardian are non-Catholic, there must be a founded hope that the child will be raised Catholic (cf. c. 868, §1, 2°). The reception may be effected by the celebration of the Rite of Bringing a Baptized Child to the Church; the minister of the rite is a priest or deacon. However, use of this rite is optional. The juridic act that constitutes the essence of the reception of an infant is the manifestation of the intention of the parent(s) or guardian that they want their child to be a Catholic and be raised in the Catholic faith. Thus, the reception is effected by a written or an oral declaration before the competent authority by one or both parents or the guardian that they want their child to be a Catholic and that the child will be brought up in the Catholic Church. The declaration may be implicit, for example, when the Catholic parents notify the pastor of their child's baptism by a non-Catholic minister and ask to have the baptism recorded in their own parish baptismal register. Implicit in this request is the intention to raise the child in their own Catholic faith; the registering of the baptismal information is proof of the pastor's witnessing this implicit declaration.[16]

Even though the law grants the priest the faculty to confirm those he receives, the reception of the infant does not take place in the context of a rite where the infant makes a profession of faith. Consequently, the infant may be admitted to the Catholic Church, but confir-

---

[15] See also *Receive the Gift: The Age of Confirmation, a Resource Guide for Bishops* (Washington DC: The United States Conference of Catholic Bishops, 2004) 15.

[16] Quoted from the manuscript, *Liturgy and Law*, by John M. Huels, 81–82, used with permission.

mation and communion would follow later in the normal course of catechesis.

CONDITIONAL BAPTISM

The Catholic Church does not advocate the conditional baptism of those who are already validly baptized. This has been true for some time. But conditional baptism was widely practiced prior to the ecumenical movement. Just to be sure, the priest who was baptizing said, "If you are not baptized, I baptize you in the name of the Father, and of the Son and of the Holy Spirit." This formula was commonly used even for those joining the Catholic Church from churches of the Reform. Today, one hears of priests who still use it, but the practice is frowned upon.

> The sacrament of baptism cannot be repeated and therefore it is not permitted to confer it again conditionally, unless there is a reasonable doubt about the fact or validity of the baptism already conferred. If serious investigation raises such prudent doubt and it seems necessary to confer baptism again conditionally, the minister should explain beforehand the reasons why this is being done and a nonsolemn form of baptism is to be used.
>   The local Ordinary is to decide in each case what rites are to be included or excluded in conferring conditional baptism.[17]

The conditional form is to be used if there is a doubt about the fact of baptism or about its validity. In most cases, there is no doubt, and the conditional form should be avoided. When it is to be used, a "nonsolemn form" of baptism is to be followed—generally understood to mean privately and simply. Logically, the conditionally baptized adult or child of catechetical age would also receive confirmation and communion in the same nonsolemn ceremony, but it is hard to imagine how this would continue to be nonsolemn. It is best to avoid conditional baptism if at all possible. The Catholic Church's newfound aversion to conditional baptism demonstrates its acceptance of the validity of the baptisms of many other churches.

The rite of baptism does not supply the formula for a conditional baptism. This could be an oversight, or the omission may suggest that

[17] RCIA 480, citing *Ad totam ecclesiam*, 14–15: AAS 59 (1967) 580. See also CCL 869.

the conditional formula is to be used apart from the solemn Rite of Baptism. Or it may imply that the formula for baptism and conditional baptism is the same. Instead of beginning with the words, "If you have not been baptized," the minister may use the standard formula: "I baptize you in the name of the Father, and of the Son, and of the Holy Spirit."

If the fact of the baptism cannot be proven or the validity of the baptism cannot be verified, the person in question could be solemnly— not conditionally—baptized. This solution presumes that there was no baptism.

A valid baptism requires using the precise words ("I baptize you in the name of the Father, and of the Son, and of the Holy Spirit"), immersion or pouring of water, and the intent to do what the church does. If a minister changes the words to something like "I baptize you in the name of the Creator, the Redeemer, and the Sanctifier," the baptism is not valid. If a minister uses the right words, but does not mean what the Catholic Church means by them (as is the case of the Church of Jesus Christ of Latter-Day Saints), the baptism is not valid.

Baptisms in the following faith communities are not considered valid by the Congregation of the Doctrine of the Faith: Christengemeinschaft (The Christian Community) of Rudolf Steiner,[18] Swedenborgiana (The New Church of Jerusalem) of Emmanuel Swedenborg,[19] the Mormons (Church of Jesus Christ of Latter-Day Saints),[20] the Free Catholic Church in Holland (Vrij Katholieke Kerk),[21] Jehovah's Witnesses,[22] and the Unitarians.[23] The Congregation also lists these communities that do not baptize: Quakers, the Salvation Army,[24] and the Church of Christ Scientist.[25]

Other groups whose baptisms are commonly deemed invalid by the Catholic Church—though they are not named in the documents from

---

[18] "Notificatio," AAS 83 (1991) 422.

[19] "Notificatio," AAS 85 (1993) 179.

[20] "Responsum ad propositum dubium," AAS 93 (2001) 476.

[21] Prot. N. 2112/58M.

[22] "Privilege-of-the-Faith Case Involving Two Baptized Jehovah Witnesses (S.C. Doct. Fid., 4 April 1966) Private," Canon Law Digest 6 (1963–1967) 651–658.

[23] Prot. N. 1271/84M.

[24] Prot. N. 1250/70.

[25] Prot. N. 2353/65M.

the Congregation of the Doctrine of Faith—include the Apostolic Church, Christadelphians, Pentecostal Church, the People's Church, and any evangelical group baptizing in the name of Jesus (not the Trinity). Also not found in CDF's documents are the Bohemian Free Thinkers and the Masons, neither of which practice baptism.

CONFIRMATION

Confirmation today is called a sacrament of initiation, even when it is deferred from baptism.[26] It was not always this way. Throughout history the word "initiation" was used only for liturgies of baptism. "Throughout the early period of the church, whenever the fathers employed the term 'initiation' they had in mind the entire baptismal complex, especially its relationship to the eucharistic mysteries."[27] Confirmation and the first sharing of communion had long existed apart from baptism, but detached from baptism they were not considered "initiation rites" until the twentieth century. The decree that opens the confirmation rite states, "In the sacrament of confirmation . . . the initiation in the Christian life is completed."[28] More precisely, confirmation does not complete initiation, but it is one of the rites (together with communion) that complete it.

Confirmation was added to the rite of reception after the Second Vatican Council. Prior to that time, the circumstances when a priest could confirm were limited. So a baptized person who joined the Catholic Church was probably baptized conditionally, and then brought to the bishop for confirmation at some later date.

However, in the reforms of the council, priests were given the faculty to confirm those they received into the church, and confirmation became part of the rite of reception. Advantageously, this permitted the newly received person to enjoy the gifts of the Spirit before communion. However, the ritual has to walk a fine line to keep from being offensive. It "completes" the communion that the Catholic Church regards as somehow deficient, and it fills the new Catholics with the Holy Spirit, making them eligible to share the Eucharist. Although the liturgy no longer includes the repudiation of heresy or absolution from the sin of heresy, it does include elements that resemble reconciliation:

[26] E.g., *Catechism of the Catholic Church*, 1212.
[27] Turner, "Double Meaning," 490 (see chap. 4, n. 6).
[28] Sacred Congregation for Divine Worship, *Decree*, Prot. N. 800/71.

handlaying and prayer for the coming of the Holy Spirit. These have a positive meaning—the gift of the Spirit. However, the sacrament is conferred because of the Catholic belief that ecclesial bodies without a valid presbyterate do not have valid confirmation, and that the gift of the Spirit needs to be given the baptized who have an insufficient status in the church. Within the Catholic Church, those baptized as infants are not required to be confirmed before they receive First Communion. But for those baptized in other churches, confirmation helps seal one's reception into the full communion of the Catholic Church, and it precedes First Communion.

The situation is different for those joining the Catholic Church from an Orthodox Church. In their case, no confirmation is given. In the Orthodox Church the priest who baptizes also confirms. The Catholic Church recognizes the validity of his ordination and of the confirmation he administers. Hence, the sacrament is not repeated for Orthodox Christians joining the Catholic Church.

Confirmation is one sacrament with several different meanings in the Catholic Church. It is celebrated together with the baptism of adults as part of one initiation rite. It is deferred from the baptism of infants and celebrated as a kind of maturity ritual. It accompanies the rite of reception for those without a valid confirmation. In that form it carries the joy of the gift of the Holy Spirit, but it also lays bare the disparity of Christian churches yearning to be one.[29]

Some people preparing for the rite of reception feel that confirmation should not be required of them. They were confirmed in their own tradition, for example, where their confirmation indicated their readiness to live out their commitment to Christ. That ceremony held special meaning for them. To be confirmed again would seem to cast a shadow over the value of the commitment they thought about and ratified. But Catholic confirmation means something else. It is a gift of the Holy Spirit upon the baptized. Even though many teens who celebrate confirmation are told in so many words that this is their lifelong commitment to the Catholic Church, there is nothing in the ritual that says so. They renew their baptismal promises, but they essentially do this every time they recite the Creed at Mass. The sacrament of confirmation is conferred with the words, "Be sealed with the gift of the Holy Spirit." Confirmation is about the gift of the Spirit.

[29] See Turner, *Confirmation: The Baby in Solomon's Court*, revised and updated (Chicago: Hillenbrand Books, 2006).

If candidates for the rite of reception object to confirmation on the grounds that they are already committed to Christ, a careful explanation may help: These are two different ceremonies with the same title. It is not about a commitment to Christ; it is about the gift of the Spirit. If candidates object on the grounds that they have already received the Holy Spirit in baptism, it can be argued that the Spirit comes to the faithful in many ways, and this way holds special meaning for Catholics. One can also say that the Catholic Church believes the ecclesial status of candidates is incomplete. These are not warm words in ecumenical conversation, but they do indicate where the church stands.

BAPTIZED, UNCATECHIZED CATHOLICS

Some baptized, uncatechized Catholics desire to receive the sacraments of the church. The American edition of the Rite of Christian Initiation of Adults has grouped them together with baptized, uncatechized Christians of other faiths[30] and expanded the rituals that may demarcate the stages of their catechetical process. The question that drives the catechesis is not why one wishes to switch to Catholicism, but why one wishes to receive the sacraments.

In some parts of the world, the number of such Catholics is quite large. The baptism of infants is regarded as a social event more than a religious one. It gives families an opportunity to join together after the birth of a child, and to give some assurance of their desire to hand down the faith to a new generation.

However, many parents who ask for the baptism of their new child do not follow through with raising the child in the practice of the faith. Children grow up without the catechesis expected of those approaching the sacraments of reconciliation, confirmation, and Eucharist. If later in life they seek to become active again, they are candidates for confirmation and communion. They are not received into the full communion of the Catholic Church because they are already members.

Confirmation preparation may take various forms. In practice, some people prepare very simply, learning what the sacrament means and preparing to renew their baptismal promises. Others undergo a longer program if the parish or diocese feels that the candidates should be given a more extensive period of time to learn the basic Catholic catechesis they did not receive earlier in life.

[30] RCIA 400.

In some dioceses, confirmation preparation is part of marriage preparation. Confirmation is strongly encouraged but not required of those to be married,[31] probably because of the unavailability of bishops in some parts of the world. Some dioceses make confirmation a requirement for marriage, even though they cannot justify it from the universal law.

[31] Code of Canon Law 1065/1.

Chapter 10

The Clouded Vision in the United States

SECTIONS 4 AND 5

The adaptations inserted into Part II, section 4 of the 1988 English translation of the Rite of Christian Initiation of Adults in the United States have clouded the vision of the rite of reception in section 5. All well-intentioned and approved by the Vatican, the adaptations of catechumenate rites for baptized candidates have managed to disaffirm the baptism received, especially when celebrated in the combined rites.

The English translation of the entire RCIA was freely adapted from the Latin original. The Latin has 392 paragraphs treating the rites of initiation and an additional 31 paragraphs for the rite of reception. The English translation spans 597 paragraphs plus several appendices. Most of the nearly 200 additional paragraphs deal with the adapted and combined rites.

Pastoral experience had shown that those who were approaching the Catholic Church for sacraments had similar stories of faith, whether or not they had been baptized. So a parallel series of rites was created, lest those who were already baptized feel excluded. These rites also alerted the faithful to their role of prayer and support of both catechumens and candidates.

James Dunning believes that the adapted rites affirm the baptisms of those being received because without them the ritual seems sterile:

> [D]o we really respect Protestant baptisms by an understanding of sacrament which minimalizes the connection between sacramental rites and faith? Was not Protestantism birthed by reformers who *protested* that minimalism? Did they not rail against magical rites

in which God supposedly acted and changed us regardless of the
faith of the person, the ministers, or the community?[1]

But the additional adaptations obscured the original vision of the
rite. Far from offering combined rites for catechumens and candidates,
the *Ordo initiationis Christianæ adultorum* presented a series of prebaptismal and initiatory rites for catechumens and only one rite for the
baptized candidate: the rite of reception. Uncatechized Catholics were
considered separately from candidates for reception. There were no
special rituals for baptized, uncatechized Catholics because they would
follow the usual rite of confirmation, and receive First Communion on
any Sunday when they were ready. Furthermore, the rite of reception
for those baptized outside the Catholic Church was not conceived as
part of the Easter Vigil. It was to take place at some other time of year,
preferably during Mass, even a Sunday Mass, as the need arose, candidate by candidate.

This simple approach to the reception of baptized candidates shows
the influence of the ecumenical movement over the history of reconciling heretics. The council's idea was to compose a new ritual for the
new ecumenical climate.

The American adaptations changed all that. Part II, section 4 of the
English translation, "Preparation of Uncatechized Adults for Confirmation and Eucharist," was originally composed for baptized, uncatechized *Catholics*—not for members of another Christian community.
It envisioned persons baptized Catholic in infancy, but never brought
up in the faith. The text says that their high point "will normally be the
Easter Vigil,"[2] a decision for which there was no historical precedent.
The Easter Vigil had always been reserved for baptisms in the early
church. Liturgical books of the Middle Ages still included the rites of
initiation at the Easter Vigil, but they were infrequently used. There is
no evidence that previously baptized Catholics received confirmation
or communion from bishops at the Easter Vigil. Perhaps in the excitement of restoring the catechumenate and Holy Week, the framers of
the *Ordo initiationis Christianæ adultorum* rolled previously baptized
Catholics into the same ceremony. RCIA 409 offers no further explanation. It appears to be an innocent suggestion, hedged by the word
"normally."

---

[1] Dunning, "What Is a Catechized Adult?" 4 and 6 (see chap. 5, n.12).
[2] RCIA 409.

The same paragraph continues with these remarks about the Catholic baptized in infancy but only now completing catechesis in preparation for the sacraments:

> At that time they will make a profession of the faith in which they were baptized, receive the sacrament of confirmation, and take part in the eucharist. If, because neither the bishop nor another authorized minister is present, confirmation cannot be given at the Easter Vigil, it is to be celebrated as soon as possible and, if this can be arranged, during the Easter season.[3]

This paragraph does not say "they are received into the full communion of the Catholic Church," because they are already in the full communion of the church by reason of their Catholic baptism. The authorized minister of their confirmation is the bishop, not the priest. The priest has the faculty to confirm those whom he receives into the church, but the bishop is the ordinary minister of confirmation for one who is baptized a Catholic. This paragraph makes sense only if the section is treating Catholics, which was its original purpose.

That purpose was changed by the insertion of a phrase in the American edition. The first paragraph describing the preparation of the uncatechized now says this:

> The following pastoral guidelines concern adults who were baptized as infants either as Roman Catholics or as members of another Christian community but did not receive further catechetical formation nor, consequently, the sacraments of confirmation and eucharist.[4]

The American edition inserted this phrase into that paragraph: "either as Roman Catholics or as members of another Christian community," which changed the meaning of the paragraphs that followed. It is still speaking about the extreme condition of those who "did not receive further catechetical formation, nor consequently, the sacraments of confirmation and eucharist," but many parishes interpreted it to mean virtually all baptized candidates.

The adapted rituals were inserted next: the rites of Welcoming, Sending, the Call to Continuing Conversion, and the Penitential Rite.

---

[3] RCIA 409.
[4] RCIA 400.

These were added to section 4, redesigned for anyone baptized with relatively little Christian upbringing. But the rites have been used quite extensively—not without some benefit to individuals—but at some cost to their understanding of the significance of the baptism they have received.

Because section 4 had been composed for the formation of baptized and uncatechized Catholics, no climactic liturgy appeared there. Candidates finished their preparation with confirmation by the bishop and then communion. Section 5 appropriates the appendix to the *editio typica*: the Rite of Reception. The American edition of the *Rite of Christian Initiation of Adults* conflated the intent of the two sections, setting up section 4 as if it were the preparation required for section 5. The newly created rites for baptized candidates were thus included in section 4, the meaning of which was adjusted to include those validly baptized outside the full communion of the Catholic Church.[5]

To survey the contents of the book, it looks as though the rituals of Part II, section 4 are preliminary to Part II, section 5, the Rite of Reception. They may be, but they need not be. They are always optional. Even an *uncatechized*, baptized Christian may skip the rituals of section 4 and be received into the church, after catechesis, with section 5.

Kathy Brown writes of the rite of reception, "The instructions for the rite do not say why a person would celebrate this particular rite rather than participate in the extended pastoral formation intended for catechumens or baptized, uncatechized adults."[6] But the reason is the significance of their baptism. Ron Oakham characterizes section 4 as the part for "baptized, uncatechized Christians" and section 5 as the part for "baptized, catechized Christians."[7] It can be read that way. However, that was not the original principle of the divisions between sections 4 and 5. Section 4 was intended for Catholics and section 5 for other Christians. The purpose of section 4 in the American edition was expanded to include other Christians who were uncatechized. Section 5 remained untouched. Section 5 is for every baptized Christian who wants to become Catholic, regardless of their level of catechesis. Each one should be catechized before being received. Not all require the same amount of catechesis.

---

[5] RCIA 400.

[6] Kathy Brown, "Expanding the Limits of Initiation," in *One at the Table*, 8.

[7] Ron Oakham, "Normative Dimensions of Initiation," in *One at the Table*, 145.

The North American Forum on the Catechumenate offers institutes and workshops to help those in parish ministry prepare catechumens and baptized candidates.[8] Its flagship institute, Beginnings and Beyond, offers participants a weeklong immersion in the rites, structure, and catechesis of the Rite of Christian Initiation of Adults. Its primary focus is the formation of catechumens. The Forum offers another institute called Concerning the Baptized. Below is an excerpt from a chart the Forum shares with participants.

Who Path	Baptized Christian uncatechized (little or no previous religious formation)	Baptized Christian with significant religious formation
Ordinary path	Extended process, using all rites in Part II – 4 + 5 (US 400, US – NS 30; CAN 376)	Simple process; Rite of Reception Part II – 5 (US 473 / CAN 387)
Alternative path	Shorter process, adapted rites Part II – 4 + 5 (US 400 / CAN 376) (US 473 / CAN 387)	Shorter process, adapted rites Part II – 4 + 5 (US 400 / CAN 376) (US 473 / CAN 387)
Extraordinary path	Simple process; Rite of Reception Part II – 5 (US 473 / CAN 387)	

The chart is accurate, though not clear. The rites in Part II, section 4 are always optional, even for the uncatechized Christian. This is noted only as an "extraordinary path." Baptized Christians with significant religious formation would generally not undergo the rites of Part II section 4, but could if they seemed worthwhile. Many candidates seem happy, even moved by the adapted rites. But the rites are obscuring the message of the validity of baptism.

[8] http://www.naforum.org/.

The adapted rites for candidates have no prehistory. Throughout the annals of receiving the validly baptized, there is no evidence for candidates being welcomed by a parish community, sent to the cathedral for a call to continuing conversion with the bishop, assigned a penitential rite during Lent, or being received at the Easter Vigil. All these liturgical steps are new. They were intended to help, but they have made the process more cumbersome than it ever was before.

Maxwell Johnson writes of this problem, "the adult catechumenate as envisioned by the RCIA is *prebaptismal* in nature and orientation and *not* designed with the reception or transfer of Christians from one ecclesial tradition to another in mind. Nevertheless, . . . both real catechumens and other 'candidates,' . . . are often joined together within the same catechumenal process."[9]

The RCIA encourages the dismissal of catechumens after the Liturgy of the Word at Mass,[10] but nowhere recommends the dismissal of baptized candidates. They are to remain with the other members of the Body of Christ. Yet Oakham calls the rite "ambiguous" on this point. "It says neither that they should be [dismissed] nor that they should not be. The reader can infer, however, that the preference is toward that they should not be."[11] He cites a different point of view in the Canadian edition, which says, "Candidates for reception into the full communion of the Catholic Church are invited to leave the assembly together with their catechist, in order to reflect further upon God's word."[12] Oakham encourages a dismissal of the candidates at least during the weeks before Easter as a participation in a "paschal fast."[13] But this is unheard of in ecumenical norms, which encourage the participation of Christians at common prayer as much as possible. "Prayer in common is recommended for Catholics and other Christians so that together they may put before God the needs and problems

[9] Maxwell E. Johnson, "Let's Stop Receiving 'Converts' at Easter," in *Worship: Rites, Feasts, and Reflections* (Portland: Pastoral Press, 2004) 88.

[10] E.g., RCIA 67.

[11] Oakham, "Formation of Uncatechized Christians," in *One at the Table*, 93.

[12] The adapted Rite of Welcoming Candidates for Confirmation and Eucharist says, "Candidates for reception into the full communion of the Catholic Church are invited to leave the assembly together with their catechist, in order to reflect further upon God's word" (485). *Rite of Christian Initiation of Adults* (Ottawa: Canadian Conference of Catholic Bishops, 1987).

[13] Oakham, "Formation of Catechized Christians," 133–34.

they share—e.g., peace, social concerns, mutual charity among people, the dignity of the family, the effects of poverty, hunger and violence, etc."[14]

Although the adapted rites have been gratefully received and experienced by many baptized Christians, they have set up arbitrary stations on the way to the communion table where the baptized more imminently belong.

THE EASTER VIGIL

The tendency to celebrate the rite of reception at the Easter Vigil has also changed the nature of the rite of election and the season of Lent. Many dioceses use the combined rite of election and call to continuing conversion in order to include all those preparing to join the church in the same celebration and to enter a prayerful Lent. But the rite of reception is not bound to Easter, and the call to continuing conversion is not bound to Lent. Besides, the call to continuing conversion is a ceremony adapted from the rite of election and combined with it in a further adaptation. Its presence makes the significance of the election of the unbaptized difficult to grasp. They are being "elected"—that is admitted among the new "chosen people." They enter the desert of Lent on their exodus toward the waters of Easter. But this is obscured by celebrating the rite in tandem with another one which calls the baptized candidates to continuing conversion—something which the entire community embraces on Ash Wednesday each year.

The result turns the celebration into a diocesan ceremony for those planning to join the Catholic Church at Easter—a time for them to meet the local bishop. But the rite of election links catechumens with the God of the covenant, the Exodus from Egypt, and the determination to fix one's heart on Christ. It sets the stage for the conversion of heart that will be stoked by the scrutinies. The elect signify the single-minded decision for Christ, the call to holiness, and the promise of new life. They are examples of conversion for the entire community of the faithful—including the baptized candidates—all of whom look to them to be their models during Lent.

It is good for the newly received to pray with the bishop, but it would be far more meaningful if they could do so while participating at Eucharist with him later on.

---

[14] Directory for the Application of Principles and Norms on Ecumenism, 109 (see ch. 5, n. 20).

During Lent, the scrutiny rites are celebrated explicitly for those who are unbaptized, yet some parishes adapt the scrutinies with texts that include the baptized candidate as well.[15] However, the scrutinies are prebaptismal rituals aiming to solidify the choice of those who are converting from a life outside the Body of Christ to a life centered on Christ as a member of his Body. The baptized candidate is there already. Adapting the scrutinies continues to blur the distinction between catechumens and candidates. It also participates in the rhythm that makes Easter the day for the rite of reception.

Celebrating the rite of reception at the Easter Vigil has put the ceremony at some cross-purposes with the ecumenical movement. Catholic leaders were trying to stop the conditional baptizing of those who were validly baptized and to simplify the access of baptized Christians to the table. The rite of reception was created for a typical parish Mass. But the adapted liturgies for baptized candidates in the United States extended the public liturgical celebrations of those already baptized, hosted one of them at the cathedral under the presidency of the bishop, and placed the moment of reception in the centerpiece of Catholic liturgy, the Easter Vigil.

The tilt toward celebrating the rite of reception at Easter was firmly established by the combined rite for initiation and reception in the 1988 American edition. Even though the combined rite was placed in an appendix in the back of the book at the request of the Vatican, it gained widespread usage. Many parishes are proud of the numbers of candidates and catechumens in formation, and they take care of both groups in a single rite at the Vigil.

This is not contrary to church law. But the legislation is confusing. Speaking of uncatechized, baptized candidates (originally with Catholics in mind), the rite says, "The high point of their entire formation will normally be the Easter Vigil."[16] The National Statutes in the United States said of the rite of reception, "It is preferable that reception into full communion not take place at the Easter Vigil."[17] The

---

[15] Oakham, "Final Preparation of Uncatechized Christians," in *One at the Table*, 102. He also proposes the implementation of penitential rites in place of adapted scrutiny rites, but this solution still suffers from the problems of overly expanding the rituals required for reception and keeping Easter as the primary occasion for this rite.

[16] RCIA 409.

[17] National Statutes 33 (see RCIA Appendix III).

introduction to the combined rite says, "Pastoral considerations may suggest that along with the celebration of the sacraments of Christian initiation the Easter Vigil should include the rite of reception of already baptized Christians into the full communion of the Catholic Church. But such a decision must be guided by the theological and pastoral directives proper to each rite."[18] The introduction is of two minds as it continues:

> Inclusion at the Easter Vigil of the rite of reception into full communion may also be opportune liturgically, especially when the candidates have undergone a lengthy period of spiritual formation coinciding with Lent. In the liturgical year the Easter Vigil, the preeminent commemoration of Christ's paschal mystery, is the preferred occasion for the celebration in which the elect will enter the paschal mystery through baptism, confirmation, and eucharist. . . . The celebration of their reception at the Easter Vigil provides the candidates with a privileged opportunity to recall and reaffirm their own baptism. . . . [T]he baptismal themes of the Easter Vigil can serve to emphasize why the high point of the candidates' reception is their sharing in the eucharist with the Catholic community for the first time.[19]

However, the introduction cautions, "The decision to combine the two celebrations . . . should, then, be consistent in the actual situation with respect for ecumenical values and be guided by attentiveness both to local conditions and to personal and family preferences. The person to be received should always be consulted about the form of reception."[20]

Oakham argues in favor of celebrating the combined rites:

> The celebration of a new union is real for baptized Christians who have been catechized in and shared a union with a Christian community of another denomination. Thus, the Reception in its unadapted form (celebrated outside of the Easter Vigil) is most appropriate for them. However, for those who have been baptized, but who have had no catechetical formation nor any true affiliation with another Christian communion, their celebration of reception

---

[18] RCIA 562.
[19] RCIA 563.
[20] RCIA 564.

is far more an experience of profession of Christian faith within the full communion of the Catholic Church. To this end, the rite's combined form, set within the initiatory context of the Easter Vigil, is more appropriate for the uncatechized Christian. The rite in its combined form, while celebrating a new union, highlights a new commitment of faith with its renewal of baptismal promises and an encounter with the baptismal waters through the sprinkling rite which are so much a part of the Easter Vigil celebration.[21]

References to not celebrating Reception at the Easter Vigil are in the context of the pastoral formation of baptized *catechized* Christians, while references to doing so are in the context of the pastoral formation of baptized *uncatechized* Christians. For the uncatechized, the initiatory context of the Easter Vigil may be appropriate because this will most likely be their first real response of fidelity to their baptismal commitment (something the baptized catechized Christian has already been doing as part of his or her ongoing faith journey).[22]

However, to some degree, every candidate comes uncatechized and undergoes catechesis. Candidates are all received after they have been sufficiently catechized. The level of their previous catechesis is immaterial to the time of their reception.

Strong arguments can be made in favor of keeping these celebrations separate. As Johnson puts it,

> Let's stop receiving "converts" at the Easter Vigil so that the Easter Vigil *and* the Lenten catechumenate itself can function properly in relationship to baptismal preparation and renewal in a way consistent with its origins and with the primary intent of its modern restoration. In so doing, let's all take seriously the preference of the *National Statutes* in order that any and all ecumenical confusion about baptism be avoided. Quite simply, there is neither historical precedent for the reception/confirmation of baptized Christians from other traditions at *Easter*, nor any sound *theological* reasons why such *should* take place. If anything, the theology of *baptism* itself mitigates against such a practice and it is *baptismal*

[21] Oakham, "The Reception of Baptized Christians: Ritual and Pastoral Considerations," *Institute Resource Packet*, 49.

[22] Oakham, "When Do We Celebrate Confirmation with the Baptized, Uncatechized Catholic? A Continuing Conversation," *Catechumenate* 27/5 (September 2005) 21–22.

theology—not convenience and not some vague notion of inclusivity—that must shape pastoral practice at this point.[23]

If not Easter, when should baptized candidates be received? When they are ready. The rite of reception makes no connection between its ceremony and any time of the liturgical year. Weddings happen when the engaged couple is ready. Priests are ordained when they are ready. People confess their sins when they are ready. The sick are anointed when they are ready. Other Christians become Catholic when they are ready.

[23] Johnson, "Let's Stop Receiving 'Converts' at Easter," 90–91.

Part V

Conclusions

The Rite of Reception of Baptized Christians into the Full Communion of the Catholic Church fulfills a need for those who are baptized in other communities and are eager to live as Catholics. The ceremony composed after the Second Vatican Council has been freed from past implications that those joining the church are sinners in need of abjuring heresy and experiencing reconciliation. It has been replaced with a ritual of much friendlier tone, honoring the baptism already received, while taking the candidate through the simple steps of professing faith, being received into the church, confirmation, and communion.

In parishes, good work is being done to prepare Christians for this transition. They learn what the Catholic Church teaches. They experience the community of Catholics. They participate in service opportunities. They join in the worship of God. Those already married to Catholics experience new unity at home, new peacefulness, and a joint commitment of belief expressed in the ways they live.

The ecumenical movement of the twentieth century has made the Catholic Church more sensitive to other Christian bodies. In effect, the Catholic Church has changed its opinion of these bodies from being circles of heresy to "ecclesial communities." This more respectful term recognizes the unity that exists on some level because of a shared baptism.

Still, more progress can be made. Christian church bodies are yearning to be one. Among the churches of the Reform, there exists considerable agreement on baptism and its implications. Those who are baptized are usually admitted to the eucharistic table even without membership in the host ecclesial body. Such Christians transfer memberships through simple ceremonies of welcome, without any abjuration from the past, formal acceptance of local doctrines, or ceremony of handlaying and anointing. Communion may be shared, but it may be shared even before the baptized person becomes a member.

The Catholic Church remains in dialogue with other churches and ecclesial communities. The issues are quite different from one dialogue partner to another. The Catholic Church believes that the sharing of communion depends on adhering to a system of beliefs, not just on baptism. Baptism makes one a part of the Body of Christ, but Catholic communion depends on something more.

Many individual Catholics wish the church would exercise more hospitality toward other Christians wishing to share communion. After all, many other Christians invite Catholic visitors to share communion at their worship services.

The ecumenical movement of the twentieth century succeeded in shifting the winds. Prior to that time, Christian churches seemed more interested in differences than in unity. Relationships among these bodies are now marked by greater courtesy and zeal than ever before. The communion tables are not all open, but this progress should be acknowledged.

The Catholic Church needs to continue fervently its dialogue and to seek ways to retain respect for its own teachings while building stronger bridges to other Christian communities. Progress would tremendously change the rite of reception. If entire ecclesial communities could be gathered at one table, individuals would not need to undergo the rite of reception. The Catholic Church faces criticisms. Many Christians think a valid baptism should allow access to Catholic communion. If the Catholic Church accepted that premise, it would pursue a liturgical plan similar to that of other Christian churches, in which reception into full communion would not be necessary because full communion would already exist; and confirmation would not be necessary because sufficient gifts of the Spirit would have been acknowledged in baptism. Differences will always exist, but must they keep Christians from a common table? If they did not after the apostolic era, must they do so today?

The separation among Christians today is different from the separation that existed after the apostolic age. In those days, Christians were dealing with real heresy, especially around the person and nature of Christ. It was in that environment where today's rite of reception had its antecedents: when reformed heretics sought reception and reformed apostates sought reconciliation.

But that is not the case today. The rite of reception today is the fruit of the awareness that baptism is the foundation of unity. A baptized Christian is seen differently and is received differently. The Catholic Church is not yet at a place where it regards all baptized Christians eligible for communion, but the camps are not as far apart as they were centuries ago.

Catholic parishes can do more to recognize this progress. Well-intentioned efforts at including baptized candidates in the preparation and celebrations for catechumens have backfired. A love for the liturgy and a recognition of its power have inspired the creation of additional ceremonies for candidates that were not envisioned in either the liturgical reform or the ecumenical movement. When Catholics bring candidates through a series of rites prior to their reception, they mean to enliven the worshiping faith of the community, but they succeed in polarizing the baptized from the baptized. By including the rite of reception into the framework of the Easter Vigil, Catholic parishes blur the distinction between the baptized and the unbaptized. They confuse the meaning of the very baptism they are trying to exalt. They verge on the triumphalism that the church was trying to avoid.

The vision of the reception of validly baptized Christians is much simpler. The liturgy is not meant to be protracted nor sensationalized. It has some business to do. What happens is something marvelous—the sharing of the Spirit in confirmation and of Christ in communion. But within the context of what baptism is, who the Body of Christ is, and what the ecumenical movement has been trying to achieve, it can be handled simply.

By celebrating the rite of reception at the Easter Vigil, Catholic parishes are actually taking back some of the steps they had gained in the ecumenical movement. Although other Christians are no longer baptized conditionally, they are brought into the church at a ceremony highly charged with baptismal imagery. It is hurting the mutual recognition of baptism that Catholics and other Christians have worked so hard to attain.

Baptized Christians who wish to join the Catholic Church should be given every courtesy and assistance. They need information about and experience with the Catholic Church. And they need a simple ceremony, the rite of reception, which could be offered to them as soon as they are ready, preferably on a Sunday in the presence of the local community. By granting them this respect, Catholics will build on the strong foundation of baptismal unity, and they will help erect a church in which communion becomes not only easier to achieve but more visible in their midst.

Bibliography

Brand, Eugene L. "The Lima Text as a Standard for Current Understandings and Practice of Baptism." *Studia Liturgica* 16 (1986) 40–63.

Duggan, Robert D. "A Response to Andrew M. Greeley." *America* 161/10 (October 14, 1989) 235–37.

Dunning, James. "What Is a Catechized Adult?" *Forum Newsletter* 9, no. 3 (Summer, 1992) 1, 4, 6.

Greeley, Andrew M. "Against R.C.I.A." *America* 161/10 (October 14, 1989) 231–34.

Johnson, Maxwell E. "Let's Stop Receiving 'Converts' at Easter." In *Worship: Rites, Feasts, and Reflections*. Portland: Pastoral Press, 2004, 83–94.

Journey to the Fullness of Life. Washington DC: United States Conference of Catholic Bishops, 2000.

Lienemann-Perrin, Christine, ed. *Taufe und Kirchenzugehörigkeit: Studien zur Bedeutung der Taufe für Verkündigung, Gestalt und Ordnung der Kirche*. Munich: Chr. Kaiser Verlag, 1983.

Marchal, Michael H. "'No Greater Burden': Celebrating the Reception of Already Baptized Christians." *Catechumenate* 28/1 (January 2006) 32–35.

Oakham, Ronald A., ed. *One at the Table: The Reception of Baptized Christians*. Chicago: Liturgy Training Publications, 1995.

Pontifical Council for Promoting Christian Unity. *Directory for the Application of Principles and Norms on Ecumenism*. Vatican City: 1993.

Rite of Christian Initiation of Adults. Study Edition. Collegeville: Liturgical Press, 1988.

Root, Michael and Risto Saarinen, eds. *Baptism & the Unity of the Church*. Grand Rapids: William B. Eerdmans, 1998.

Sieverding, Dale J. Ordo admissionis valide iam baptizatorum in plenam communionem ecclesiae catholicae: *An Historical Study of the Ritual Aspects of Reception into Full Communion with Special Attention to the Adaptations of the Rite for Use in the Catholic Church in the United States*. Rome: 1997.

———. *The Reception of Baptized Christians: A History and Evaluation*. Forum Essays 7. Chicago: Liturgy Training Publications, 2001.

Turner, Paul. *Ages of Initiation: The First Two Christian Millennia*. Collegeville: Liturgical Press, 2000.

———. "The Double Meaning of 'Initiation' in Theological Expression." *"Imaginer la théologie catholique", Permanence et transformations de la foi en attendant Jésus-Christ: Mélanges offerts à Ghislain Lafont*. Ed. Jeremy Driscoll. *Studia Anselmiana* 129. Rome: Centro Studi Sant' Anselmo, 2000, 487–99.

Wilson, Stephen G. *Leaving the Fold: Apostates and Defectors in Antiquity*. Minneapolis: Fortress Press, 2004.

Index